"At last—a concise, readable, biblical guidebook for improving parent-teen communication. Borthwick brings his many years of experience working with teens and their parents to bear with honesty, frankness, and best of all, compassion. This is a 'must read' for parents of teens and soon-to-be teens."

—Noel Bechetti
Editor
Youthworker Journal
El Cajon, California

"Paul Borthwick is one of the country's most creative, conscientious youth workers It is evident from this book that he has drawn not only upon his extensive study of the theory of adolescent growth and development, but also upon his many years of effective practice of those theories. Anyone seriously concerned about developing healthy relationships with teenagers will find this book most helpful. Communications with teens is such a high priority on the agenda of the church that this book will go a long way toward helping youth workers and parents achieve that goal."

—James W. Reapsome
Executive Director
Evangelical Missions Quarterly
Wheaton, Illinois

"The issues dealt with in this book are on the cutting edge of youth ministry and these are the kinds of issues that I am faced with in counseling and dealing with students and parents every day. Paul gives a biblical, sensitive, and warm treatment of some practical solutions to parent-student problems. There are some fresh ideas in this book. While Paul gives some sensitive and personal applications, he remains objective because of the wide experiences he brings to this book in working with many students over the years.

"This is a good book, well written, that I highly recommend to parents."

—Ridge Burns
Pastor of High School Ministries
Wheaton Bible Church
Wheaton, Illinois

"Borthwick gives solid advice on the *everyday* problems faced by parents of teenagers. In some ways, that is a bigger challenge than dealing with acute crises. It is in the day-in and day-out jousting over issues like honesty, morality, trust, and forgiveness, that Christian life patterns are shaped. I recommend Borthwick's book highly."

—Terry C. Muck
Editor
Leadership Journal
Carol Stream, Illinois

But You Don't Understand

But You Don't Understand

Paul Borthwick ⟨1954–⟩

A Division of Thomas Nelson Publishers
Nashville • Atlanta • Camden • New York

Copyright © 1986 by Paul Borthwick

All rights reserved. Written permission must be secured from the publisher to use or reproduce any part of this book, except for brief quotations in critical reviews or articles.

Published in Nashville, Tennessee, by Oliver-Nelson Books, a division of Thomas Nelson, Inc., Publishers, and distributed in Canada by Lawson Falle, Ltd., Cambridge, Ontario.

Scripture quotations are from the NEW KING JAMES VERSION. Copyright © 1979, 1980, 1982, Thomas Nelson Inc., Publishers.

Letter to Ann Landers reprinted by permission of Ann Landers, News America Syndicate, and the Boston Globe.
Quotations from the book *Let's Succeed With Our Teenagers* reprinted by permission of Jay Kesler.
Chapters 2, 3, 4, 9, and 10 originally appeared in the *Alliance Witness* and are reprinted by permission.

Quotation from Jacques Ellul's *Money and Power* published by Inter-Varsity Press is reprinted by permission.

Quotations from Jim Stafford's book review copyrighted by Christianity Today 1984 and used by permission.

Quotation on page 46. Jane Norman & Myron Harris, Ph.D., excerpted from *The Private Life Of The American Teenager*. Copyright © 1981 Jane Norman & Myron Harris, Ph.D. Reprinted with the permission of Rawson Associates.

Printed in the United States of America.

Library of Congress Cataloging-in-Publication Data

Borthwick, Paul, 1954-
  But you don't understand.

  Bibliography: p.
  1. Adolescence.   2. Adolescent psychology.
3. Parenting—Religious aspects—Christianity.   I. Title.
HQ796.B6845   1986   305.2'35   86-2348
ISBN 0-8407-9540-8 (pbk.)

Contents

Foreword

When I was much younger, I assumed that hard work meant doing something physical, such as stacking hay bales or painting a house on a hot day. As I grew older, I began to realize that hard work could also mean doing something mental or emotional, such as sitting at a desk making decisions or listening to people who had come to share desperate problems.

But it occurs to me now that it is also hard work to be a parent, to enter into all the multiple operations it takes to create and maintain a climate in which children can grow from infancy to adulthood. That's why a book like this one is important. It focuses on the issues and processes of the hard work in the home where mothers and fathers have only so many years to turn "barbarians" (as someone has indelicately put it) into responsible citizens.

I have known Paul Borthwick for years and have watched him develop the insights contained in this valuable book. I can vouch for his credibility because I watched the man grow out of his own adolescence and work his way through college and graduate school. As his pastor I helped disciple him through his call to ministry, united him in marriage to his lovely wife Christie, and laid hands on him when it came time to ordain him to the work of the pastorate. As a team leader, I approved the decision to call him to the Grace Chapel (Lexington, Massachusetts) pastoral staff as minister to youth. As a friend, I stood next to him at bedside and embraced him as he watched his father die. Through all of that, I've come to believe in him and in what he says.

Perhaps there's another, even more personal, reason why I am convinced that Paul's thinking is worth the reader's attention. Paul was youth pastor to my two children, Mark and Kristy. I listened to their comments to one another and to their mother and me about Paul and his youth program at Grace Chapel as they were experiencing it. I have this suspicion that they would have died for him. They appreciated the way he taught them the Bible; his approachability when there were questions; his frankness in speaking the truth. They took note of his steadiness, his practicality, his vision.

One day, as I entered Paul's office to confer with him on a business matter, I noted a chart on the back of his door. The chart was marked with scores of names, each followed by a series of check marks in various columns. It was his way of keeping track of the spiritual growth and development of young people over a multiyear period. My own two were on that list. I knew Paul was husbanding a dream for each of them.

The power of Paul's book lies in its usefulness for everyone who has responsibility for raising children, especially single parents who have the awesome task of playing both mother *and* father to young people.

And there are more and more of that sort of person in our world.

The fact of the matter is that raising teenagers is indeed hard work. Demanding, challenging, sometimes exhausting. But very, very rewarding. I know. I've seen and experienced the payoff. Part of the credit for that payoff in the lives of our children belongs to Paul.

I'm proud to introduce Paul Borthwick's first book to readers. There will be many others to follow because God has put His hand upon the author. And as a parent I've felt the effect.

Gordon MacDonald
President, Inter-Varsity Christian Fellowship

Preface

My observations recorded in this book are largely due to the open, growing people of Grace Chapel in Lexington, Massachusetts. Over the past ten years, I have worked with these teenagers and their parents, and as a result, I have had hundreds of opportunities to observe what makes parents more or less effective with their teenage children.

Not being a parent of teenagers myself has actually had its advantages. Since I am not preoccupied with one or two teenage children (as parents can be), I have had the opportunity to observe many families in action. I have counseled with young people whose relationship with their parents is superlative, and I have met with others who are contemplating running away because relationships are so bad at home.

The Grace Chapel families have included the broad spectrum of family situations: single-parent homes, homes in which one parent is not a Christian, and conventional homes. Some teenagers in our group have been rebellious toward parents and God, while others have been remarkably receptive.

It is to all of these teens and their parents that I owe this book. They have allowed me to learn from them, and they have been willing to share growth experiences with me, many of which I pass on to you in these chapters. Since I have dealt with sensitive material here, some of these case histories are composites of actual people and events to protect the privacy of those involved. In several cases, I have changed names to protect the privacy of the people with whom I work. Thus, while the characters and names are fictitious, the conversations I record did occur.

I also am indebted to Gordon and Gail MacDonald. They have been excellent examples as parents to their two children, Mark and Kristen. I have come to know both of their children through the youth ministry here at Grace Chapel, and I have learned much from their relationships as parents with teenagers.

Finally, I am grateful to my wife, Christie. She has been the most perceptive observer of teenagers and their relationships with parents. Through her involvement in the youth group and in the intense environments of three-week youth-mission teams, she has been able to learn about the stated (and hidden) reasons why parents and teenagers are growing well together. She has drawn the teenagers into conversations that reveal their true feelings about their parents. She has been the insightful one who has taught me many of the principles stated here. She has encouraged me to use these principles in my work with teenagers, and as a result, I have been a better youth leader.

The insights offered, therefore, are not all mine, but are the result of many people's experiences with teens. It is my hope that the compiled observations will serve readers who desire better, healthier relationships with young people.

Paul Borthwick

Introduction

Why another book on parents and teenagers? After all, there already seems to be a plethora of books on the subject. Consider, too, that statisticians tell us the teenage population in the United States is actually waning—and yet questions remain.

When I talk to parents of teens, they say, "Bring on the books! We need all the help we can get." This is especially true when it comes to the matter of *communication* in the home. This is an area in which many parents are asking for help.

"My kids don't talk to me as much as they used to." This parent wonders if things are starting to break down at home.

"I don't have the foggiest idea of what to talk about with my teenager," says another parent. "Can you give me some ideas, and can you help me know how to get into those conversations?"

"Whenever I talk with my teenager, we always seem to end up in either an argument or a stalemate. Is there a solution?"

Probably all parents wish for the principles or keys that can guarantee 100 percent success with their teenagers. We would all love to find the magic buttons that, when pushed, yield healthy teens who converse with parents, look to parents for advice, and always turn out as well-adjusted, mature adults. Unfortunately, no such magic buttons seem to be available. There are no methodologies that guarantee success.

A humorous solution attributed to Mark Twain describes his way of guaranteeing success with teenagers:

- At age thirteen, seal the teenager in a barrel and leave a hole at the top for air and for the sending of food through a straw.

- Then, at age sixteen, plug up the hole!

Many parents will pass through a period of time when they wish that they *could* "plug up the hole." Frustration with teenagers is not uncommon. Their unpredictable behavior and their adolescent viewpoints can, at times, drive parents crazy.

But most teenagers *are* open to growth and change. Actually, their entire worlds are full of change—changing styles, changing bodies, changing educational environments, changing outlooks on the world and the future. The fact that teenagers are open to change is the why of this book. Teenagers are open to (and even desirous of) positive changes at home. They want positive relationships too.

That is why this is written primarily for parents. Parents can be the positive change-agents in the home. They are the ones who can direct the home so as to maximize the growth of all family members.

These chapters are designed to get parents thinking about *qualities* (love, respect, honesty) that can build a rapport between themselves and their teenagers.

The *values* (responsibility, freedom, morality, forgiveness) are addressed because they must be established from parent to teenager. These chapters offer suggestions on *character traits* (discernment, convictions, trust) that parents should seek to build into their teenage son or daughter.

Admittedly, crisis issues in the world of today's teenager are not dealt with here. References are made to teen pregnancies, teenage runaways, suicide, and the like, but few remedies are discussed. That is because this book is intended for the so-called average home, the home in which relationships are not at a point of crisis, but they are not what they could be.

But You Don't Understand is designed to build preventative maintenance into the relationships of parents and their teenagers. The guidelines offered are for parents who want to build relationships so that crises do *not* occur. The hope is that parents who desire to make the years of adolescent growth positive for the teen and the entire family will be able to implement these concepts to make the relationships healthier and more productive.

As a youth worker, I have observed that *parents* truly make the greatest long-term difference in the life of the teen. Personalities, qualities, character traits, and values are passed down from one generation to another. For this reason, my efforts as a youth minister must be at least, in part, directed to the parents.

It is *you,* the parent, who makes the greatest difference in the life of your teenager and in the life-style you will share at home. Thus, these chapters are designed to give you some ideas as to how to make more of a difference in the most positive directions.

Why Teenagers Can Be Hard to Love

Teens Are Hard to Love

I know because I was a teenager, and I was hard to love. Rebellious language, long hair, and sloppy clothes were my outward expressions of the inner turmoil and confusion that accompany growing up. For my parents, siblings, and friends, I made myself hard to love.

Danny (age fifteen) is the son of the pastor. Their relationship is only mediocre, and it is getting worse. The main reason? Danny acts out some mild rebellion by horsing around during the morning service every Sunday. His father finds Danny very difficult to love.

Beth (age seventeen) told her folks that she did not want to come to church anymore. Although her mother and father have accepted that decision with some hesitation, they are growing in their impatience toward their daughter because she has started drinking with her friends. They suspect that she is getting drunk, but they do not know what to do. "Do we kick her out of the house?" they ask. "Or do we just hope that the problem resolves itself?" They are wondering what it means to love her.

Glen (age fourteen) is a fairly passive teenager, but he loves his music. His parents do not mind the music as much as they mind the appearance that Glen has adopted along with his music. He wears a punk hair-style (shaved on the sides, bushy at the top), and he has just had an ear pierced. His father (who had always hoped that Glen would become a lawyer) despairs; his mother calms the father by saying, "It's just a stage that he's going through," but inside, she wonders what is going on in Glen's head. What does it mean to love him?

Yes, teenagers *are* hard to love. Just as Mother or Father is thinking, *Ah, my child is finally growing up to be a mature young person,* the teen does something out of character. He says something that seems like an intentional effort to cause problems in the home. She does something that seems irrational, and the parent wonders, *Do I know my child?*

The Well-Known Signs

Teenagers are hard to love partly because they *are* teenagers. Their bodies are changing, and they will adopt unusual behaviors, like spending hours in front of the mirror worrying about pimples, nose size, eye shape, or future baldness. They change their clothes styles to adapt to their short-tall, fat-thin perceptions of their bodies. Even their metabolism can make them hard to understand and difficult to love. "Why is my kid energetic during church services and lethargic when it comes to working around the yard?" "How come my daughter can never sit still for more than five minutes?" "Why are our quiet nights at home never quiet now that Benny is age thirteen?"

Their life-view is also changing, which can make them difficult to love as well. They will fluctuate from wanting to be a child (dependent on the parent) to aspiring to be an adult (independent). They will be helpless at times and express no desire for independence, and at other times, they will resent any efforts from the mother or father to help them.

As growing young adults, they will want to think their own thoughts and make their own decisions, but they are often ill-equipped to do so. As a result, they will act stupidly. They will make statements that seem incredibly immature to their parents, and yet teenagers will flare up at any implication that their perspective is juvenile. At the time of their lives when they most need adult guidance and advice, they will be most resistant to receiving it.

Teenagers are hard to love, but it is the atmosphere of love created by the parents that will make growth possible. Although loving parents will be anxious to help teenagers grow, they will also recognize the challenge of helping in such a way that it neither belittles the teenagers nor makes them defensive.

My parents did a good job of loving me. They tolerated me through my stages of defensiveness and insecurity. They bounced back and forth with me as I debated becoming a civil engineer on one day but wanting to run away to Montana on another. They demonstrated their love by not giving up and by seeing me through my teen years (and beyond).

1 Corinthians 13

To understand love for teenagers, we are wise to look to the Scriptures first. There we find the instructions for how to love and the Source of such love—the Lord Jesus Christ.

First Corinthians 13 defines *agape* love, love that is undeserved, love without reciprocation from the one loved. It is this love that caused God to send His Son to love us sinners. It is this love that is needed by parents who desire to love teenagers (who can indeed be "unlovely" at times). First Corinthians 13 points us in the direction of love as well as to the power Source, and it defines the specific attributes of godly love that can be applied in relationships—in this case, in the relationship of parent to teenager. Let's consider just a few of these attributes of *agape* love as they apply to parents with teenagers.

"Love Suffers Long"

Patience. When Mrs. White returns home from her job (which she took so that her son, Steve, could have some financial possibility of going to college), she finds that Steve has not done any of the dinner preparation she asked him to do; patience is in short supply. Her first reaction is to blow up at Steve, telling him that he is "ungrateful," "inconsiderate," and "a very selfish young man."

Mrs. White's words may be true, but her manner of presenting them may be incorrect. Although she is upset, she probably would have done better to ask a few questions. Maybe Steve was detained at school. Maybe her instructions were unclear. A patient response by Mrs. White could have at least explored the whole story. Now, Steve is on the defensive, and it is unlikely that objectivity can be restored.

Parents need patience to enable them to understand the teenager. When the teen's love seems to be leaving them, parents need patience to try to understand why. Perhaps the teen is growing to the point where he is redefining his expressions of love. Maybe daughter does not want to kiss Dad in public anymore; maybe son is embarrassed to death when Mom says, "I love you," in front of his athletic friends. Maybe Mom and Dad need to be more patient in finding out how their teenager feels rather than worrying about their own feelings.

Patience is also needed when a rift seems to be developing between parent and teen. Patience in this respect may mean forgiving the teenager's unjustified criticisms of the parent. As Dr. David Elkind points out in his book *All Grown Up and No Place to Go*, teenagers are entering into thought processes that allow them to dream and idealize. As a result, they are able in their teen years to imagine "a world of peace and harmony, a perfect church, and a perfect family." Why do they become so critical? Dr. Elkind says it is because of "their ability to imagine ideal parents against whom his or her real parents suffer by comparison" (p. 28).

Almost every person can remember the tumultuous discovery that other people's parents were "better" than his or her own. As a teenager, I compared my parents with Mr. and Mrs. Bailey (who were much less strict), Mr. and Mrs. Collins (who *never* made their kids go to church), and Mr. and Mrs. Sousa (who were always giving their children lots of spending money). As a result of my naive and idealistic comparison, my parents came out as the losers.

Patient love means allowing for conversation and exploration to mollify situations and to explain the actions of teenagers so that parents can *respond* rather than *react*. For parents, patient love means forgiving, listening, and caring for teens in terms they can understand.

"Love Is Kind"

The love God has for us is such that He treats us in the ways we need to be treated instead of the ways we *deserve* to be treated. The idea is that of *mercy*.

The greatest action of kindness of parent to teenager is manifested by perseverance. In spite of hurts caused, failures, and even active rebellion, the parent refuses to give up. The parent refuses to retaliate. That's why I made it. My parents were not perfect, but they never gave up.

Mrs. Christopher is kind in her love for her daughter, although her daughter has caused her great pain. There have been malicious words, open rebellion, and even threats. When she sits in my office, I ask Mrs. Christopher why she has not asked her daughter (now almost eighteen) to leave home. Her tear-filled eyes reveal that she has probably thought about it, but she responds, "No, I could never do that. My daughter is very angry, but her anger will not be solved by my carrying out my anger toward her."

Most cases are not quite as drastic as this one, but they still have to do with the idea of retaliation. The kind parent does not humiliate his teenager's lack of life-knowledge by public embarrassment. The kind parent does not look at arguments as win-lose situations. Rather than see parent-teen conflicts as struggles in which the superior parent must exert authority over the presumptuous teenager, the kind parent sees these struggles as opportunities to understand, teach, and love that teenager.

"Love Does Not Envy"

Perhaps nothing is sadder than seeing parents and teenagers in competition with each other. It happens sometimes at our parents' nights in the youth group. As fathers and sons play volleyball, the fathers may start to become defensive. Their skilled and agile sons are winning with ease. The winded (and sometimes overweight) fathers are feeling humiliated; they have something to prove. Thus, the competition gets tough. Fathers start arguing the plays; sons start exerting a good feeling of superiority; and the spirit of fun is lost.

Envy. Jealousy. Pride. These feelings are all possibilities between parent and teenager. When the son or daughter enters the teen years, these feelings can become most apparent. A father sees that his son is getting to be more athletic or brighter or more popular as a teenager than he ever was when he was in high school, and envy arises. The father—either subtly or directly—starts to look for opportunities to win over his son because he desires to maintain a superior position as the father.

The same can be true of mothers and daughters. One mother may be envious of her daughter's beauty. Another may see her daughter on a career track that she could never pursue, and there may be jealousy or envy over the life options that are available to the daughter.

The book *Is There Life After High School?* by Ralph Keyes, observes that the high school experience in America is one of the most important factors in determining our ideals as adults. For those who failed in the intense high school world, there can be a desire to overcompensate in adult life. All of this points to one fact for parents: Be careful not to compare your teenager's achievements with your own success or failure in high school. Let each teen grow as an individual.

Parents who desire to love their teenagers must make a concerted effort to win over envy or jealousy. Love from the parents should mean the willingness to rejoice in the success of the teenagers, even if it is greater than that of the parents.

"Love Does Not Parade Itself"

Mr. Berg is having difficulty with his son, Larry. Mr. Berg (B.A., Yale; M.B.A., Harvard; Ph.D., Boston University) is very success oriented. He loves Larry, but he desperately wants Larry to have more drive, more initiative. Larry has initiative, but not in the areas that Mr. Berg calls "real life." Larry wants to be an artist, and he cares little about "income-earning potential." Little by little, he is growing away from his father. It is not so much the fact that his dad has other goals for him (in private conversation, Larry admits that his view of the artist's life is not too realistic); it is the way that his dad has started pounding his own success into Larry's head. Mr. Berg—in his attempt to motivate Larry—has been emphasizing again and again *his* past successes, *his* financial prosperity, and *his* educational accomplishments.

Mr. Berg's efforts to motivate his son through comparison will not work. Larry will grow best to be a mature young man only when he sees that his father loves him—whatever he turns out to be. His father's boasts of his own past successes only make Larry feel that "I could never be as good as my father, so why should I even try?" Perhaps this is why Larry is aiming at a field so distinctly different from his father's.

Loving teenagers does not mean boasting about our successes to show them how wonderful we were as teenagers. Such boasting—although it may prompt the competitive few—may actually discourage most teenagers from trying. Love means accepting teens where they are and then seeking to affirm and encourage them by recognizing what they do well. The parent who seeks to love his son or daughter does so not by making comparisons, but by allowing the individual to grow into special God-given skills and abilities.

"Love Is Not Puffed Up"

Are you willing to be wrong? Are you willing to learn from your teenagers? If your answers are yes, then you have learned what it means to be "not proud" or "not puffed up." The loving parent knows how to admit that he or she has failed and sinned

27

(we'll discuss this later in the chapter on forgiveness). The loving parent sees the parent-teen relationship as a mutually growing experience; therefore, being educated by the teenager is enjoyable.

Some parents, unfortunately, are too proud and self-concerned when it comes to relating to their teenagers. They see conflicts as an us-against-them battle. They are afraid to learn about the teenage world of today because they are fearful that their stereotypes will be demolished. When they fail, they somehow manage to blame their children or some other external force; they are unwilling to accept personal blame.

There is freedom when pride is put aside. Parents who are able to rebound from failures and who are willing to learn from their young people are free. They can know joy in their relationships with their teens, and they can communicate a mutual respect (see Chapter 2) that will help the relationship flourish.

Love is not puffed up. And neither is the parent who loves.

Other aspects of 1 Corinthians 13 love will be pursued in later chapters. Chapter 9 is directed at the need for us as parents to trust our teenagers and—on a higher plane—to trust God. Chapter 10 discusses the challenges of forgiving both ourselves and our teenagers.

It is a great challenge for parents to love their teenagers with this *agape* love. Teenagers are hard to love in the first place, and *agape* love intensifies the challenge because it requires the giver to love without thought of reciprocation.

In practical terms, a parent who desires to love a teenager with *agape* love should ask one basic question: How does my teenager *need* to be loved? God knew us in our sinfulness, and He knew what we needed; therefore, He sent Jesus in response to our need for love and forgiveness. A parent should evaluate a teen's needs from this same perspective—love and forgiveness.

Some Questions to Consider

The following questions can help you respond with selfless, giving love to your teenager:

- Do I need to do some reading about adolescent characteristics so that I know what my son or daughter is experiencing physiologically or emotionally? (This can help you understand the growth stages your teen will go through.)

- Am I talking enough with my teenager so that he knows I care? Am I spending enough time with him so that he would open up and talk if he had something to say?

- Am I being consistently impatient, unkind, proud, or boastful in my relationship with my teenager?

- Where is my teenager with respect to self-image and self-concept?

Is he *insecure* and in need of my encouragement?

Is he *full of anger* about past experiences?

Is he *in need of space* so that he can experiment with adult decision making and responsibilities? (See Chapter 3.)

Is there any area in which my teenager *needs to experience my forgiveness and assurance* so that he can start afresh?

Is my son or daughter *feeling a comparison* with what I was when I was a teenager? (Am I projecting this comparison through my attitudes or actions?)

These are questions for evaluation that can be used between husband and wife or between parent and teenager. When I have shared questions such as these with parents at Grace Chapel or with parents who have attended parent/teen seminars that I have conducted, the most frequent response has been, "But how do I find out how I am doing with my teenager?"

How Are You Doing? Ask!

Teenagers are perceptive and can offer some good, honest answers if they know that you are willing to listen. Remember to hear their answers, but also remember that their answers are their teenage perceptions of reality. Nevertheless, you may find out that your teenagers have more to say than you gave them credit for. When you hear where they are coming from, you will find yourself more equipped to love them as they need to be loved.

Why Teenagers Don't Seem to Respect Parents

The Rodney Dangerfield Syndrome

A mother and her teenage son walk out of a department store, the mother loaded with bundles. As she crosses the street, she stumbles and drops a package. The son picks it up but remarks sharply, "Ma, you are such a klutz."

A father (a teacher in the youth Sunday-school class) starts to speak about the day's lesson, but he is distracted when he realizes that his daughter is leading the back row of girls in a chorus of snickers and giggles.

Each parent might inwardly or outwardly ask this question: *Why doesn't my teenager respect me?* Perhaps there is nothing quite so frustrating and, at times, humiliating to parents than to be on the receiving end of the disrespect of teenagers. Sassy language, inattentive ears, or rebellious behavior all speak to parents of one basic message: *My kids do not respect me.*

Various parents respond differently to such disrespect. Some try harsh discipline and even physical punishment, but this often yields further bad behavior on the part of the young person. A spanking or a slap across the face for disrespectful language has a diminishing effect as a teenager grows older.

What Can Be Done?

Although there are no easy solutions to this problem, parents can work toward building respect in the home by respecting their teens. Mutual respect is important in any healthy relationship, and that is no less true for the relationship between parents and teenagers. Parents want respect, but teens may fail to give it. Yet teenagers often show disrespect to their parents because they feel that their parents show disrespect to them. Did your teenager ever say to you, "Why do you always treat me like a baby?" Maybe your teenager has perceived some of your actions as being disrespectful to him. These feelings of disrespect on both sides can lead to a loss of communication, and a parent/teenager conflict is the result.

Mutual respect within the home is essential for at least two reasons. *First,* it is *biblical.* In Ephesians 5:21 (the verse that introduces Paul's teaching for husbands, wives, parents, and children), we are exhorted to submit "to one another in the fear of God." The Ephesian Christians probably did not have older teenagers at home; most of them would already have been married. Nevertheless, Paul sets forth teaching on relationships by commanding that all involved start by submitting to each other in reverent respect for the other person's value in God's eyes.

Second, it works. As a youth minister, I have seen hundreds of young people and parents interact, and it is apparent that the most successful families are built on mutual respect. When a teenager comments, "I love my parents because they listen to me," or a parent states, "My kid has some great ideas; you should hear him out," I can see the respect within the home.

I saw this respect in action in my own teenage experience. From a positive viewpoint, I can remember how important I felt when my parents would consult my opinion on a decision. But, negatively, I can also remember the feelings of hurt or anger that rose within me when my mother or father would state (or imply), "What do *you* know? You're only a kid!"

Respect Defined

The matter of respecting one's children can be misunderstood and can lead to disaster in the home. Some parents interpret it this way: "You should not disagree with your teenagers. Let them have their own way. Do not squelch their developing sense of independence."

How wrong! Respect does not mean that we allow our teenagers to have their way all the time. Nothing is further from biblical standards. Parents should be trying to produce responsible young adults, not emotionally babied teenagers who are crushed whenever they do not get their way.

The type of respect that parents can provide so as to produce healthier relationships in the home can be defined in this way:

A fundamental belief that my teenager is a human being, precious in the sight of God, capable of thinking, and in need of my coaching as his/her independence develops.

Parents need to believe that their teenagers are human beings. Maybe I am supersensitive because I work with teenagers, but it seems to me that many adults think that teenagers are animals that should be caged from age thirteen to eighteen. Indeed, the intense physical, emotional, and intellectual growth that occurs during these years may make us think that teens are uncivilized, but they are young *people* who are growing up.

Parents need to believe that their teenagers are precious in God's sight. In spite of their emotional fluctuations, and in spite of their confused perspective on life, teenagers are recipients of God's mercy. God remembers that we are "but dust" (see Psalm 103:14), and teenagers (who are sometimes "dustier" than we want to admit) are precious in the eyes of a merciful God.

Parents need to believe that their teenagers are capable of thinking. Granted, their thoughts may be immature and reflect their limited life perspective, but if thinking is to be encouraged, parents must learn to filter out the profound thoughts that are there.

Parents need to be *coaches*. Teenagers do not need a mother or father who acts and thinks like a teenager.

They need *models,* examples of faith. Respect does not mean that everyone acts and thinks on the same level. Parents are put into a superior, authoritative position by God, and they should act accordingly.

Seven Suggestions For Building Respect

If parents want to build this respect within the home, where do they start? Here are some practical suggestions to consider:

1. *Listen.* Perhaps nothing is more important to a teen and his attitude toward his parents than his knowledge that they want to listen to him. Listening, however, might become very difficult for tired, harried parents, especially when both parents are working. Nevertheless, parents must work at *active* listening, not just from behind the newspaper or in front of the television.

"But my kids never want to talk!" Every parent knows the experience of asking 1,001 questions of a teenager only to get a "yup" or "nope" answer to every one. The frustrating part of listening to teenagers (trying to show interest in their world) is that they sometimes do not talk. Perhaps some of these suggestions regarding respect will create more talkative environments.

2. *Take teens' lives seriously.* Let's examine a common situation. Jane Smith is thirteen years old, just finishing grade seven. She comes home to her mother one day and explains that she is in love with the boy she wants to marry, Richie Jones. Mother Smith lis-

tens intently (a good thing to do!) and reminisces with Jane about her first love (also okay to do). Jane goes out for a while, and when she returns home, she hears her mother on the phone with a friend: "Oh, Ruth, the cutest thing happened today. Janey came home with her first puppy love, and she's convinced that he's the man for her. Isn't that adorable?"

No matter what the mother thinks from her perspective of thirty-five years, she has just crushed Jane. To the mother, the experience is "cute," "puppy love," and "adorable," but to Jane at age thirteen, it is a serious matter. In six months, when Jane has another intense experience, she will be reluctant to share it with her mother because her mother did not respect her confidence. She will think, *She does not take my life seriously. She thinks I'm just a little girl.*

Parents do well when they look back on their own teenage years. The intensity of relationships, the crisis of failing a test, the humiliation of getting cut from the team, and the pressure to follow peers are earth-shaking issues to teenagers. Parents show that they care about and respect their teenagers when they try to understand the importance of these issues to their young son or daughter.

3. *Come into the teen's world.* "Oh, Dad, you are so out of it!" Did you ever hear this? Indeed, parents frequently are out of touch with the teenage world of the eighties. The parent's thought is often, *Things were tough when I was a kid too,* but that does not help in relationships with today's teenagers.

The parent who wants to communicate love and respect will make a concerted effort to go into the world of his teenager. Imagine the effect of a father asking a son if he could meet him at school for lunch! Or what would happen if parents agreed that they would split the choice of radio stations fifty-fifty when they drive on vacation, allowing the teenagers in the family to select the station half the time?

Some will respond, "But my kid wants me to leave him alone. He sees me in public and ignores me. I go to his football games, and he's embarrassed." All of these things happen, but wise parents will know that the outward responses of teenagers are not always reflective of their true feelings. They may be outwardly embarrassed to have parents in their teenage world, but inwardly they love and need the support that is being offered.

In my sophomore year of high school, I played on the sophomore football team (a team for those who could not make junior varsity). The team did not get many people at the home games, but my mother was always there.

Every home game, we would skulk out of the locker room, trying to look tough. As we passed the bleachers, my mother would be there waving at me. Inside, I would cringe with two fears. First, I was afraid she would yell out, "Hi, honey!" in front of my teammates; second, I feared that if I got injured, she would rush onto the field.

Neither of my fears was realized. She just came to the games, talked to the other parents, cheered when we scored, and went home. She wanted to come into my world for a while to let me know she cared. And, in spite of my football toughness, I noticed and was glad that she was there.

4. *Allow for disagreement.* Many parents are uncomfortable when their teenagers start thinking for themselves. They perceive it as being their failure to train their children correctly: "If I had done the right thing as a parent, my kids would never think this way."

Parents who can overcome this false sense of guilt can grow alongside their teenagers in the midst of questions, disagreements, and even constructive arguments. When a teenager asks, "Why do we believe in God?" be willing to sit down and discuss it. Do not give the pat replies; if the teenager asks, he or she is probably searching for an answer.

Teenagers and parents can also disagree about more perfunctory things—hairstyles, clothing, music, and so forth. Parents, be simultaneously firm in your own convictions and yet flexible to change on matters that are not really too important. Just because "we have *always* done it that way" is not usually enough of an answer for the searching, curious, inquiring minds of teenagers. Show that you respect them by answering their questions thoroughly; you do not always need to agree, but you do need to try to give an answer for the convictions by which you live and run your family.

5. *Learn to let go.* In addition to feeling frustrated by the differences of opinions that teenagers voice, parents are at times anxious because they see their teenagers drifting away from them. "My son does not want me to kiss him anymore," a father grieves. "My daughter told me to stop calling her Janey; she wants to be called Jane." A mother is stunned to see her little girl grow up.

For the parents who can remember the birth of their child, the first day she walked, the first day he talked, the child's teenage years are a frightening realization that they are growing older. As the children choose their own friends, decide on their futures, and make choices that the parents do not always approve of, the parents are tempted to cling to the past. Although rationally they know they must let their children go, they are emotionally hesitant.

Parents, if you want your teen to become an effective, responsible young adult, you must endure changes. Clutching will cause pain for both you and your teenager. There must be a letting go of the child into God's care, trusting that your love and God's goodness will bring him back to you by his own choice.

6. *Be respectable.* Parents who respect their teenagers, and who want their teenagers to respect them, will try to be respectable. In the teenage years (in spite of superficial opposition), young people want to be proud of their parents. They want to be able to present Mom and Dad with an air of dignity that says to their teachers, friends, and coaches, "They belong to me!"

Being respectable has to do with a parent's ability to be consistent in the Christian life. It has to do with how the parent presents himself or herself in public. It has to do with a parent's ability to lead by example. Teenagers are seldom proud of or respectful of the parent who lives by a "do as I say, not as I do" double standard.

7. *Get God's perspective on yourself.* Many parents are disrespectful and overbearing toward their teen-

agers because they themselves are not at peace with God. They fail to have a merciful attitude toward teens because they do not know God's mercy toward themselves. They do not forgive because they do not know the forgiveness of God.

For parents to respect and care for teenagers, they must start with their personal relationship with God. Knowing that God loves them will help the parents love their teenagers. Experiencing the forgiveness of God through Christ will empower them to forgive the failures of their children.

Rx *for Respect*

"My kids do not respect me." Is it true? Maybe it is, but the remedy can start in the home when the parents of teenagers begin to show respect toward their children. When parents build relationships on the fundamental belief that their teenagers are human beings, precious in the sight of God, capable of thinking, and in need of their coaching, there will be improvement in the growth between parents and teenagers. As they see that their parents respect them, teenagers will offer their respect in return.

Why Dependent Teenagers Need Independence

Is my teenager an adult or a child? Should I treat him like an adult when he sometimes acts so immaturely? Should I give her adult privileges when she seems so unwise?

If these questions plague the parent of a teen, imagine how confused the young person feels: Am I an adult? Why do I do some of these stupid things? Am I a grown-up or not?

The question of adulthood/childhood is what makes the teen years very difficult. A thirteen-year-old girl has the maturity of a child in the body of a woman; a teenage boy wants to be a mature man, but his perspectives are, at times, quite naive.

Importance of Developing Independence

If parents are to be effective in addressing these questions, they must be willing to confront the problem head-on and help their teenagers grow into adulthood. The key word is *responsibility!* Effective parents teach their teenagers to be responsible about life.

Many parents, however, shy away from this concept. "My kids are too young." "Why deprive them of their fun years?" "If I give them responsibility, they will surely blow it!"

Jay Kesler, the president of Youth for Christ, addressed this problem in his book *Let's Succeed With Our Teenagers:*

> If there is one overriding problem that seems to be evident to all people who work with teenagers today, it's not the neglect of parents for their young people, it's the tendency of parents to be over-protective and to keep young people from growing into independence. One of the most typical situations is the parent who says, "My son went away to college (or the army) and they ruined him."

> The truth is, the young person goes away from home and becomes exactly what he really is when the props are removed. Young people have the perfect right to make choices, and we cannot protect them from it. One of the most basic aspects of the parent relationship is understanding that the task of parenthood is to develop independence, not dependence, in our children. To rear children toward independence is one of the highest goals of parenthood (p. 32).

Developing independence is a lot easier said than done. Even the God-given parents of Jesus had great difficulty when He, at age twelve, became a "preteen runaway" (see Luke 2:41–52). Jesus was developing an independent sense of His life purpose, but it was not easy for His earthly parents because it required Him to break away from them.

If, however, as Jay Kesler states, the basic task of parenthood is to develop independence, how can it be done? And how can we simultaneously build into these teenagers the ability to be responsible as well as independent? (Most parents have little trouble seeing their teenagers grow in independence; the dilemma is helping them develop responsibility at the same time.)

Before we proceed to some practical suggestions for building independence and responsibility in teenagers, let's add a final brick to the foundation of this concept. Some parents may object: "Kesler's words were written over ten years ago; these are more difficult times, and we have to be more protective of our youths. If we don't, they will become 'secularized.' Too many of their peers have full independence and responsibility, and they cannot handle it."

These objections are, in part, true, but we must always be cautious not to overcompensate one extreme (such as teenagers having too much responsibility and freedom) by going to another ("tightening the grip"). There is a balance, and this balance can only be achieved when parents accept the fact that they are called—as parents—to train their children to grow into responsible, independent young adults. Overprotective parents will yield one of two results in teenagers: they will become rebellious toward the well-meaning parents, or they will accept fully the overconcern of the parents and will enter the world of adult responsibility unprepared. Neither extreme is desirable.

Six Areas in Which Responsibility Can Be Given

Some parents are happy to give independence and responsibility, but the teenager does not want it. A teenager lives in a hostile world, and it is often easier to accept the protection of Mom and Dad than it is to go it alone in a tough world.

Nevertheless, parents who care about their teenager's growth into adulthood must communicate clearly that responsibility is part of growing up. Parents can give responsibility in at least six areas:

1. *Studies.* A few teenagers are natural students, and they study without any problems. Most, however, need a little encouragement and support. To build a sense of responsibility about studies, parents must help teens learn to manage their study loads.

What does this mean? On the positive side, parents can support students by providing quiet places at home to study. Perhaps the parents can read alongside their students so that all study together. Parents can also build a sense of pride in students by rewarding good performances and jobs well done.

On a more negative note, however, parents must let students accept that *D* or *F* if they deserve it. The parent who joins the student in blaming a teacher for a poor grade builds an attitude of "it's their fault when I fail" into the student.

Helping teenagers accept responsibility for their studies means that parents are willing to get involved in the lives of their sons and daughters. Perhaps one student is failing because he feels he is getting picked on every day in class, and he cannot stand the pressure. Perhaps another student is a *C+* not an *A* student. In each case, parents are to be encouragers—helping teenagers do their individual *best*.

2. *Money.* I was amazed when Dick, a high school sophomore, came to pay for his retreat; he paid with his own checkbook! "Is this yours, Dick?" I asked. "Yes," he said, "my parents think that I ought to learn how to manage my own checking account now so that I am more responsible for my money."

What a great idea—and why not? Many college students experience incredible problems because they go away to school without ever having learned how to manage money on their own. Why not let them learn in the teen years while you—the parent—are still around to help?

One family started sharing the household budget as soon as their oldest hit age twelve. This child and his three siblings learned as they grew how to manage money. Before age sixteen, they knew how to tithe, how to budget for large bills, and how to save. At one point, all that the parents did was earn the money and sign the checks; their children drew up the checks, balanced the checkbook, and paid the bills. Amazing? Not really, because the parents, acting as overseers and advisors, started them out young and were willing to teach the teenagers and let them be responsible.

A corollary to this issue of monetary responsibility is the matter of possessions. Teaching youths to be responsible for money also means that they learn to be cautious about the use of possessions. When a teenager gets his license and wants to drive, he *should* start paying for part of the auto insurance. When a daughter wants an expensive stereo, perhaps the wisest parent is the one who splits the cost fifty-fifty with her so that she will take better care of it when she gets it.

3. *Friends.* In the recent study, *The Private Life of the American Teenager* by Jane Norman and Myron Harris, the researchers found that 88 percent of the teenagers surveyed would "see their friends even if their parents disapprove" (p. 152). What does this say to the parent who wants to build responsibility into a teenager?

Basically, the message is that friends (perhaps the most valued asset in the world of the teenager) are going to be chosen regardless of the opinion of the parents. No matter how strict a mother or father may be about "not seeing Tommy," the teenager will continue to see him. The high school environment makes such parental restrictions virtually impossible to enforce.

A better alternative is to accept the friends that your teenager chooses. Did you ever think that your teenager might not be too crazy about the friends *you* choose? Accepting these friends does not, however, mean condoning everything that they do.

Teaching a young person to be responsible for friends means at least three things to you as parents. *First,* it means being willing to allow these friends into your house, but holding your teenager responsible for their actions when they are there.

Second, it means holding your teenager responsible for his actions—and those of his friends when he is with them. For example, if your teen is out with friends and one is caught shoplifting, they all might be taken to the police station. A parent who lets a teenager off the hook with the excuse, "It wasn't me; it was a kid I was with," has missed an opportunity to teach that young person the importance of being an "accomplice." Letting him know that he becomes responsible for the actions of his friends is a harsh but necessary lesson in life.

Finally, a teenager needs to be taught to be responsible for himself or herself. When he tries to excuse poor grades with a "none of my friends did well either," or she blames misconduct on the fact that "all of my friends were doing it too," parents must emphasize that being responsible means standing apart from friends if they are bad influences.

One more word about the matter of accepting friends. In my experience with teenagers, I have found that parental disapproval of an undesirable friend almost always ensures the fact that the teen will cling to that friend. The desire in a teenager to be independent from parents makes him take parental disapproval as a "dare" regarding a bad-influence peer. Parents are much wiser to try to be as accepting as possible of their teenager's friends. If they are, the teenager will choose friends who are more like him rather than ones who are just intended to shock Mom and Dad.

4. *Chores at home.* It may sound old-fashioned to use a word like *chores,* but young people need to know that life is not going to be presented to them on a silver platter. The mother who waits on her kids hand and

foot is making a huge mistake. What will they do when there is no one around to cook the food, clean the house, or do the laundry?

In the teen years, young people need to know how to handle the regular responsibilities associated with the basics of living. They *should* be responsible for mowing the lawn, doing the dishes, or cleaning their room.

However, this does not mean that parents should institute a "parental aristocracy" designed to make teenagers responsible for all chores. (Sometimes parents put excessive responsibilities on their teens with the explanation of "I served you all these years; now it is your turn to wait on me." This attitude usually results in an argument in which the teenager invariably responds, "I didn't ask to be born, you know.") There should be a sharing of responsibilities so that making the household tick becomes more of a team effort.

5. *Time.* Everyone has 168 hours a week in which to live and serve God. Teenagers are no exception, and an important part of growing up is learning to be responsible for the management of that time. Parents can help in a variety of ways.

First, parents can help teenagers manage time by confronting them when they waste it (but keep in mind, six hours of listening to music might not be "wasting time" to your teen). One mother chose a humorous approach to this confrontation; when she walked into her son's room and saw that it looked like Times Square after New Year's, she inquired about its messiness. "I just couldn't squeeze it into my busy schedule" was her son's response.

The mother sat on her son's bed and shook her head in wonderment. "That's amazing."

"What's amazing?" her son asked.

"It's amazing how the president can run the entire country in 168 hours per week, but you cannot squeeze cleaning your room into your busy schedule. Do you get the point?"

The son got the point, but he might not know any better ways to use his time. For this reason, parents can also help teenagers be responsible for time by teaching them how to plan a schedule. Some students will take on a part-time job, participate in extracurricular activities, and get involved at church—and then they will wonder why their schoolwork is falling behind. Caring parents need to teach teenagers how to manage time and how to say no as well as yes.

Helping young people establish schedules might mean blocking off their school schedule with them, estimating how much time they need to study, commute to school, "hang around" with their friends, and fulfill other responsibilities (extracurricular activities at school, chores at home, or part-time jobs). By doing this, parents can help their teens see where their time is going and then make some changes.

Perhaps the best way that parents can teach effective time use to their teenagers is by example. If your teen spends too much time in front of the television, are you right there the whole time too? Growing alongside your teenager in making better use of time is the best teaching tool available to you.

6. *Spiritual decisions.* Perhaps the most difficult area of responsibility and independence for parents to accept is the one of spiritual choices. I often coun-

sel parents, "When you train your children to make their own choices, they do." And oftentimes they make choices with which parents do not agree, especially if the choice revolves around Jesus Christ as Savior.

How should parents respond? As hard as it sounds, parents must learn to take the spiritual pressure off, especially as teenagers get older. Parents must resolve themselves to the fact that *forcing* teenagers to commit their lives to Jesus will result either in later rebellion or disillusionment *(Did I accept Jesus because He is the truth or because my parents made me?)* about the faith.

The best action that parents can take is to handle the honest questions of faith that arise and wait on the Lord for the teenager's decision. The natural part of growing up is the transition (usually in the teen years) of making the "faith of my fathers" one's own faith. Every person must ultimately make that decision individually, and parents must allow it to happen.

Related to this whole matter of spiritual decisions, the question often arises from parents, "Should I force my teenager to go to church (or youth group)?" I do not know. I can tell you that my parents did, and it resulted in my conversion to Christ at age seventeen. I should add, however, that my siblings were also forced to go, and they left the church and the faith as soon as they were out of the house. The answer? Each parent must prayerfully and cautiously decide before God; there is no single answer, and what works in one situation might not in another.

Four Final Steps

Building responsibility and independence is a process for parents and teenagers, but parents can take some additional steps to help the process along:

1. *Allow for failure.* Maybe your son will bounce a check if you give him a checkbook. Maybe your daughter will back the car into the garage door if she drives alone. Mistakes are inevitable, and the way you respond to these failures will mean the difference between growth in the teenager toward greater responsibility and the desire to quit.

The parent who harps on the failure and refuses to let the teenager forget ("Do you realize how much trouble you've caused me?") will communicate one basic message to the young person: You cannot do it!

The parent who realizes that failure is a part of growth, however, can turn the worst disaster into a growth experience. Forgiveness, accompanied by the willingness to let the teenager try it again, is the best method of teaching a young person to be responsible.

2. *Be willing to grow yourself.* The best way to teach young people to make good, responsible decisions about life is to provide a good example. Parents must be willing to let teenagers know that they do not have all the answers, that they fail sometimes, and that they have made bad choices in the past. When teenagers realize that the home environment is a matter of growing alongside Mom and Dad, they are much more willing to learn and develop as persons and as Christians.

3. *Be an advisor.* It is difficult to let go of children. Parents want children to do well, and they hate to see them fail. The result? Rather than stay as an advisor and allow the teenager to struggle through a tough issue or task, the average parent wants to step in and say, "Let me do that for you."

Advise, but do not take the task away from your teenagers. Letting them struggle through the difficulties is a hard but necessary lesson that leads to the healthy sense of independence they need to survive in the world.

4. *Pray.* It is a complicated world into which today's teenagers will go as responsible, independent adults. They need our prayers and the power of God.

Although most parents agree with this statement, many spend much more time yelling at their teenagers, complaining to other parents about "kids these days," or bemoaning their failure ("Where did we go wrong?") than they spend praying for their young people.

If the current generation of teens is to develop into responsible Christian adults who make wise choices, parents must provide a strong foundation of prayer.

A High Goal, Indeed

"To rear children toward independence," writes Jay Kesler, "is one of the highest goals of parenthood." By building some practical areas of responsibility into their lives, parents can facilitate this process and help their children grow. The result will be teenagers who are growing in maturity and who are prepared to face the adult world.

Why Answers Are Not Easy

I was amazed as I watched Mrs. Jason and her fifteen-year-old son as they drove through the center of town. It was a cool day so the car windows were closed, but it was obvious that they were having a serious argument. Both had animated expressions, and both seemed to be talking in louder-than-average voices.

A few days later I saw Andy Jason at youth group. After the meeting, I took him aside and asked about his relationships at home. "Oh," he said, "things are great." After a little fruitless probing, I finally asked him about the incident I had observed in the car.

"That?" Andy was amazed at my concern. "Well, Ma and I were just hashing out the question of whether a teenager should go to dances. She and I disagreed, so I guess we argued."

"What did you decide?" I asked.

"We decided that there were no easy answers, and we need to talk some more. As a matter of fact, she asked me to ask your opinion."

No Easy Answers

That experience with Andy has stuck with me, not because of the question of dancing, but because of Mrs. Jason's willingness to hash things out with her teenage son and her admission of the fact that there were no easy answers.

As I have worked with teenagers for the past few years, I have often referred to the fact that there *are* no easy answers to many of the issues in the world in which they live. The moral, ethical, and spiritual standards of our world have grown fuzzy, and the Christian teenager especially needs help in dealing with personal standards.

The problem is, however, that many of our teenagers' parents grew up in a world that was somewhat more neatly ordered. The standards may not have been clear, but there *were* standards. The church usually took a harder look at culture and often separated itself from culture. Now the separation is not as clear, so parents of teenagers do not know how to deal with the secularization of our society.

Dealing with the Secular World

The option that many parents of teenagers are choosing today—at least Christian parents who are trying to keep their children in the church—is *not* to deal with the secular world. In the frustration and confusion of a complicated society, parents sometimes choose to put on blinders to the world. They prefer to ignore the fact that there are no easy answers, and they try to continue glibly on their Christian way without wrestling with the tough questions that will inevitably confront their young people.

Parents who desire to be effective trainers and disciplers of their children, parents who aspire to have better communication in the home, must add an element of honesty to the home. The pat answers will not do anymore. To facilitate communication and to help our young people be Christians in the contemporary world, parents must admit that there are no easy answers to many of the questions being asked. Parents must be willing to take a harder, more honest look at what it means to be a Christian in the secular world. Parents must present an example of sound, Christian honesty that helps teens cope with a world approaching the twenty-first century.

But how?

These five suggestions are designed to increase a parent's effectiveness in being honest and direct about what it means to follow Jesus Christ—as a teenager or as an adult.

Five Steps to Building Honesty

1. *Discernment.* This is an age of gray areas. There are so many issues for which there are no easy answers, we sometimes get confused about what it means to be a Christian. The Christian needs discernment, and the Christian parent needs to build honest discernment into teenagers who have not yet had the opportunity to "have their senses exercised to discern both good and evil" (Heb. 5:14).

Perhaps there is no greater area in which teenagers need training in discernment than the *media.* Books, magazines, movies, television, and music bombard our youths every day, and—directly or subliminally—their values and attitudes are changed.

How can a parent be honest without eliminating the media entirely? That is a good question, especially when eliminating the media is not really an option. Young people will hear about movies (and every gory scene) even if they never go. They will hear about racy books and magazines even if they never read them. Popular songs are sung even by those who have no access to radios or tape players.

Parents can do two things to teach their children about an honest application of the Christian faith to daily living: first, *they can try to understand and observe;* and second, *they can respond with the Christian perspective.*

A concerned parent came to me and said, "My son really wants to see this movie, and I don't want him to."

"Why?" I said. "Have you seen the movie?"

"No, but I just don't want him to go."

"Well," I said, "if you want my advice, I would tell you to see it with him. If he really wants to see it, he'll find out all about it from his friends, or he'll sneak off to see it somehow. If you see it with him, you will at least know how to respond to what the movie says."

Why would I encourage this? Because parents need to understand and observe the culture in which we live before making blanket judgments or inaccurate discernments. In relating to teenagers, parents need to understand so that they can respond accurately.

Audrey's fourteen-year-old daughter came to her

with a question: "Mom, can we talk about Eddie?" (Eddie was her boyfriend.)

"Sure, honey, what do you want to talk about?"

"Sex."

At this point, Audrey told me later, she thought that she could anticipate the questions. Audrey remembered when she was fourteen and had a boyfriend; they had kissed for the first time. Audrey was sure that her daughter was going to ask about when she should kiss Eddie. But, being an honest and discerning mother, Audrey waited to *understand and observe* before *responding*.

As she listened, Audrey was somewhat surprised. Her daughter's questions had little to do with kissing. Her basic question was whether or not she should save her virginity until marriage.

Fortunately, Audrey listened. When she heard the *real* issue, she was able to answer from the Scriptures and her own experience and explain why her daughter should wait. She managed to hide her amazement at the seriousness of her daughter's questions, and she offered the honest answers her daughter needed.

Our young people need honest answers, but—before their questions can be answered—parents must find out what the questions are. Then parents can offer a biblical perspective on what it means to be a follower of Jesus Christ when one is confronted with tough issues.

2. *Understanding.* Teenagers are curious about life. They are growing up, and they have a God-given curiosity that must be understood and directed. The

questions that Audrey's daughter asked her would put many mothers into a tizzy. They might try to answer calmly, but inside they might be thinking, *Why is she asking this? Has she already gone too far? I must keep a closer eye on her.*

To be honest about the Christian life, parents must understand the growth phases through which their children are going. Dr. James Dobson recommends a father/son or mother/daughter trip in the preadolescent years to discuss puberty. Even though this trip might not solve all the problems or answer all the questions, it can set the tone in the parent/teen relationship that will enable the teenager to bring his or her curiosity to Dad or Mom rather than to a girlfriend or boyfriend.

If questions are rebuked or negated with a harsh "Why are you asking this question?" honest communication is hindered. But if parents understand their children well enough to be able to set a no-holds-barred atmosphere for questions, teenagers (and pre-teenagers) can get the correct answers they desperately need.

One parent actually confronted this curiosity issue head-on with his two preteenagers. He took them on a camping trip, and while they were together, he brought out a pack of cigarettes and a couple of cans of beer. "I know that you will want to try this stuff in the years ahead," the father said, "so I figured I would let you do it in an environment where you cannot be hurt."

The kids tried it and were repulsed and nauseated (the father told me later he had brought filterless cigarettes and strong German beer to ensure the success of the experiment). Their curiosity was satisfied, but more importantly, the father had honestly conveyed to them the fact that he understood the processes of growing up. This incident did not, in and of itself, create an honest environment in the home, but it is an indication of how honest parent/teen communication must take place.

3. *Struggle.* Mrs. Jason was willing to tell her son that there were no easy answers to the issue of a Christian dancing. The effective parent—who is willing to be honest about what it means to follow Jesus—struggles with the application of the Christian faith to daily living.

This element of honest struggle must be conveyed to young people. They do not need a presentation of Christianity that makes them run from the world in which they live. Nor do they need a worldly faith that renders itself indistinguishable from the world's ways. They need the straight and narrow way, which is following the Lord Jesus.

Following Jesus means that Christians do that which is right, that which is in accordance with the truth. Following Jesus means *commitment.* If parents communicate to teenagers that they should follow Jesus because following Jesus is the most fun, they lie. By worldly standards, and by the standards of many teenagers, following Jesus is not nearly as much fun as getting drunk, misbehaving at school, or making out.

Instead of trying to entice teenagers through a syrupy "following Jesus is fun," parents must be willing to teach and exemplify the fact that they follow Jesus

59

because He is "the way, the truth, and the life" (John 14:6). Teenagers can respond to *that* kind of honesty.

One final word about the struggle with following Jesus. In relating to teenagers, parents must be willing to struggle with the open-ended questions of faith. If there are no direct answers to certain questions, do not bluff (teenagers can detect a bluff immediately). Try to find the answers in the Scriptures or from older, wiser Christians, but if there are no definitive answers, do not pretend that there are.

4. *Consistency.* Consider two parents. Jack has three teenage sons. All of them are with him watching television. A particular show has a beautiful girl in it, and she is wearing a scanty bikini. Jack, after several minutes, says, "Well, guys, that's all for me; I cannot watch this show without lusting." He stands and leaves the room; the television is still on.

Bill has a teenage son and daughter. The daughter, Debbie, comes home with a note from her teacher telling her parents that she has been letting others copy her math homework. When Debbie responds, "Well, Dad, it was just a little thing," her father rebukes her: "God is concerned about even the little things." Later, Bill drives his son to baseball practice, and because they are a little late, he speeds. His son—who heard the discussion with Debbie—remarks, "Hey, Dad, if God is so concerned with the little things, why do you speed?"

Two parents. Both are trying to be good Christian parents, but one failed. Jack presented an honest brand of Christian obedience to which his three sons responded; after Jack left the room, they all decided that they had been lusting too, and they changed the channel.

Bill, on the other hand, presented a double-standard Christianity, a faith that said, in effect, "Do as I say, not as I do." Bill could have redeemed the situation. He could have said, "You're right, son. God *is* concerned about my speeding, and I blew it. I was a hypocrite, and I need to ask you and Debbie to forgive me."

Parents should be consistent in their example, but when they are not, and they sin, they should admit their failure and ask forgiveness of their teens. The willingness of parents to admit their failures as well as to battle the double standard of hypocrisy is the best way to teach young people what it means to be growing Christians. Teenagers need to see their parents not only as people who try to follow Jesus, but also as sinners who know how to repent when they fail.

5. *Worship.* Building honesty in the home requires that parents and children alike realize who is in charge—the sovereign God. Oftentimes, Christians seem a little hesitant to deal with tough questions or to wrestle with the inequities of life because they have such a low view of God. By their tendency to run from the unanswerable questions, Christians sometimes say (implicitly), "Let's not deal with this issue; I do not think God can handle it very well."

If this insufficient view of God is transmitted through the family, then young people—especially teenagers—will wonder if God is trustworthy. "If God cannot handle the sick people of the world, how can *I* trust Him?"

To build an honest and trusting view of God in the home (and, therefore, to build greater honesty between *people* in the home), the parents must lead the way in having a high and lofty view of God. Leading the family before God with an attitude of both humility ("All that we are or have is Yours") and honesty ("O Lord, there is so much we do not understand") will help teenagers realize that the almighty God is as much available to them as He is to their parents. It will enable them to see that Mom and Dad are in need of God's love, just as they are.

The Committed Family

Indeed, being a Christian in the eighties *is* a case of "no easy answers," but the family that commits itself to following the Lord in the midst of unanswered questions will build an environment in which teenagers can communicate regarding their concerns and needs. Teens in such homes can find parents who are honest enough and a God who is great enough to understand.

Why Discernment Is Difficult for Teenagers

Teenagers belong to what has been called the "media generation." Saturated with television, movies, videos, and music, our young people have more external stimuli than any generation before them in human history. The good news is that they have vast resources of knowledge available to them through the world of computers as well as the media, but the bad news is that the stimuli in the media is both true and false, reality and fantasy, and few adults are teaching teenagers how to distinguish between the two.

Delusions of Reality

In a community not too far from ours, two fifteen-year-old girls committed suicide together. They made a pact that they would die together, and using shotguns, they carried out the agreement. Their heartbroken parents found few clues, with the exception of one message written in lipstick on a mirror: GOOD-BYE FOR NOW.

"Good-bye for now." What could it mean? Were they

Eastern religionists who thought that they would be reincarnated to another life? Probably not. Probably they were demonstrating their own confused understanding about death. Probably they were reflecting the media portrayal of death that isn't *final*. They saw people die all of the time and then come back in other movies or on different shows. Why should they be any different?

Delusions of reality can be the effect of undiscerning minds handling the ideas transmitted in the modern media. Through seeing *and* believing, teenagers build false concepts about life, values, and even death, and their delusions lead to great *disappointment* (that life is not all they thought it would be) or total *denial* (escaping into a fantasy world where their ideas can be realized).

False images of life are communicated through music. Blue Oyster Cult (a rock group) sings a song of a young couple preparing for suicide together: The boy advises his girlfriend not to be afraid of death (the reaper), adding that Romeo and Juliet were together for eternity.

False images are communicated through the movies. Teen-genre films (*Spring Break, Caddy Shack, Fast Times at Ridgemont High,* and loads of others) advocate an immoral perception of life. One film director, Sean Cunningham, summarized life like this: "Kids get drunk, kids get laid, kids go home." (This was quoted in *Sources and Resources,* January 1985, published by Youth Specialties.)

False images—deluded ideas about life—improper values. These are the results when teenagers are saturated with the media's influence and no one corrects the ideas. Teenagers need parents who will be responsible in building discernment, teaching them how to understand the difference between truth and fantasy, between good and evil. The challenge is great, but it is possible to succeed.

Five Steps in Building Discerning Teens

Although there are no simplistic steps, there are some guidelines to keep in mind that will enable you to build discernment into your teenagers:

1. *Be discerning.* Part of the problem in communicating with teenagers about discernment is that we are brainwashed by the values and attitudes of the media. We sit and numbly absorb the statements made about life, sex, and money on television or in movies. We listen to commercials that tell us that a new car, a different cosmetic, a higher-grade soap will make us happier, more beautiful, or cleaner, and we subconsciously believe it. We can be brainwashed just as easily as our teenage children.

Honesty (see Chapter 4) is needed; parents must be willing to address the questions that are raised by movies and songs and television shows, but they must go a step further. *Parents must start by making decisions in their own lives that reflect a commitment to Christian truth and values.*

Mrs. Phillips was very upset when she came to see me. Her son, Howard, was into rock 'n' roll music, and she was fearful that he would adopt an indiscriminate life-style like that of the musicians he idolized. Her fears were substantiated, so I talked to Howard.

I learned a lot from Howard about discernment. He told me that his mother was addicted to soap operas. Should he be concerned that his mother might adopt the materialistic, promiscuous life-style of the people on the soaps? He declared "When she stops watching those soaps and stops letting their values influence her, then I will reconsider my rock music idols."

Good point, Howard. He saw the inconsistent discernment of his mother. She could be discerning with respect to Howard's music, but she was blind to the brainwashing she was getting through soap operas. Howard and his mother talked, and they both agreed that being a Christian required greater discernment. She gave up her soaps, and he relinquished his rock idols. Howard grew in perception because his mother was willing to start with herself.

2. *Tell teens the truth!* The original temptation in the Garden of Eden was the presentation of a half-truth. Satan told Eve that she would not die—and when she ate the fruit, she did not! Yet it was a half-truth. She did not die immediately, but death did enter the world as soon as the sin was committed, and eternal death became a possibility.

In the same way, the ideas of the modern media are often half-truths. For example, people with money are often portrayed as being consistently happy. I am sure that there are many happy, rich people, but the half-truth presented is that *wealth brings happiness*. This is not only contrary to the teaching of Scripture, but it is a lie!

Parents who want to build discriminating teens need to evaluate what half-truths are being presented and then address these to their young people. For instance, a teenager sees the movie *Animal House*. The undiscerning youth thinks, *Wow! Is college really like that?* The parent can intervene by explaining that there are experiences for some people in college like those portrayed in the movie, but most who live that way do not graduate and usually set a pattern for wasting their lives.

Perhaps the presentations of half-truths are most guilty of one thing: they fail to show long-term results. Teenagers spend enormous amounts of time getting drunk, seeking sex, or dodging the police in the movies. What the movies fail to show is the future effects of such living on the characters. Some get liver diseases. Others enter into unwanted marriages or feel compelled to contemplate the horrors of abortion. Others get arrested and go to jail. Fantasy endures for a short time, but reality endures for life.

Teaching young people the truth means bold conversations. I have given a talk to our young people entitled "Sex Is Not All That It Is Cracked Up to Be." In it, I explain that I am happily married and am thoroughly satisfied sexually, but I go on to explain that there is a lot of difference between sex in reality and sex in the movies. In terms they can understand, I try to let them know that if they build their sexual expectations and appetites according to what they see in the movies, they will be greatly disappointed in their relationships with their future spouses. The movies do not tell the whole story.

Telling teenagers the truth also means that we show God's values versus our world's. Teenagers have little knowledge of extended effects (after all, they have not really lived that long), so they need to be taught. The media might state that wild promiscuity yields happiness, but God advocates long-term commitment to one person. Remembering that the values we teach are from the Scripture will enable us to communicate to teenagers that we are adhering to God's standards, not just some old-time values we inherited from our ancestors.

Finally, telling teenagers the truth includes instruction in the ways of God. In a day of televised religions and potpourri of theologies expounded over the airwaves, it is easy for young people to get false ideas mixed in with the truth about how God works. When a teenager hears a statement about God from a minister, he is often not discerning enough to know if it deviates from the truth taught by his faith.

To help our young people get an idea of how there is false teaching, even in the Christian media, I give an example from my life. As a young Christian, I heard a radio broadcaster promise that if I were to give to his ministry, God would return the amount to me tenfold. I had about twenty-five dollars, so I sent it in, hoping that God would somehow send me two hundred fifty dollars soon. The next day, my car's carburetor broke, and I had to borrow fifty dollars from my father to get it fixed. Rather than a tenfold *in*crease, I had a twofold *de*crease!

Through the example of my lack of discernment, I teach our young people to look to the Scriptures to find God's values and promises. Being discerning applies even to sifting truth from falsehood in Christendom.

3. *Help them grow past peer pressure.* If we were to expound ideal Christian theology, we would probably

summarize our values like this: "What God says is *true;* what God does not say is *false*." For many teenagers, peers are put in the place of God. When it comes to values, attitudes, and even beliefs, there is a tendency for them to assert, "What *my friends* say is true; what *my friends* do not say is false."

Teenagers, as they formulate their sense of personal identity, are prone to fall prey to what psychologists call the "imaginary audience." (When he is in public with Mother or Father, the teenager is sure that everyone is looking at him and saying, "What a loser—to be out shopping with a parent!") It is the fear of this imaginary audience that makes peer opinion so strong an influence on teenagers. They conform so that they do not stand out, so that they do not make fools of themselves in front of "all their friends who are watching." Dr. David Elkind says in *All Grown Up and No Place to Go:*

> It is the imaginary audience that accounts for the teenager's extreme self-consciousness. Teenagers feel that they are always on stage and that everyone around them is as aware of and as concerned about their appearance and behavior as they themselves are (p. 33).

The greatest lesson of discernment parents can teach (and exemplify) is that *God* is our primary audience. He is the One we are supposed to please. Peer opinion cannot be downplayed as insignificant, and the imaginary audience cannot be written off as a fantasy (it is very real to teens). Instead, teenagers can be taught to discern their priorities so that pleasing God becomes the top one.

Growing past this peer pressure and discerning

that God is the audience we are to please start by example. The parent who desires to teach these things must first be committed to making God his or her top priority. Then, there must be patient teaching that empathizes with the teenager and recognizes just how hard it is to break away from peers. And, finally, there must be *support* and *encouragement* when the teenager makes the courageous decision to stand alone. When a son or a daughter stays home on a weekend night because of a decision that "the things my friends are doing this weekend would not be pleasing to God," the wise parent affirms, encourages, and even rewards such a tough choice because the teenager is learning to discern between good and evil.

4. *Talk without judgments.* In *The Private Life of the American Teenager,* the results of a survey of over 160,000 teenagers are published and analyzed. In one section, a teenage girl discusses her questions about birth control and sex. When asked why she had never asked her mother, the teenager responded, "If I brought up the subject of birth control, she would be sure I was having sex" (pp. 61, 62).

It is tough for parents to be objective about their kids. Most of us, as Tim Stafford states in a book review of *Parent and Teenagers,*

> haven't fully come to grips with the reality that most kids, male and female, graduate from high school accepting drugs as an ordinary form of recreation, having had sexual intercourse (or feeling ashamed that they haven't), and believing that their happiness is the axis on which the world ought to turn. . . . These kids

70

know things and assume things we don't; but they don't tell us about it, and they don't look to us for advice. They look to each other (*Christianity Today*, October 19, 1984, p. 59).

When teenagers actually do talk honestly with us about their worlds, we have a hard time not being shocked, embarrassed, or protective. ("Imagine, the thought of my little Johnny being subjected to such a cruel world!") Sometimes we would rather be blind to the realities of the teenagers' world than to wrestle with the perceptive responses needed.

Teaching discernment in teenagers starts when we hear them out and learn the true issues facing them. To avoid the failure of answering the questions that no one is asking, we have to *listen.*

It is talking and listening without judgment that causes most parents anxiety. It is shocking for Mother even to think of the faint possibility of her darling little boy's contemplating getting drunk. When Dad comes to grips with the fact that teenage boys could actually lust after his precious little princess, he burns with rage. So how can these things be discussed? How can parents talk with their teenagers, find out the real matters needing discernment, and then respond?

First, *tell your teenager that it is difficult for you.* Explain your subjective involvement as a mother or father. Then, ask questions. (Some find it helpful to use a contemporary book about teenagers to generate the questions. Books such as *Teenagers Themselves* and *The Private Life of the American Teenager* provide comments and statistics around which questions can be formed: "It says here that 50 percent of all junior highers have gotten drunk at least once; do you think that is true?")

When the questions are answered, try to listen without reacting. A negative reaction to an honest answer could nullify the honesty of future responses. (Your son or daughter will think, *I can see that this is just too much for Mom to take.*)

In such discussions, try to share and get explanations rather than judge and give lectures. The goal is to learn where your teenager is in the hope that you can address the values and attitudes of the Christian faith to that situation.

5. *Teach teens to think.* The impulses from the media and advertising can sometimes come at us so quickly that we fall into a state of mental dormancy. We become passive in our thinking, and our minds are put into a neutral position, to be moved in various directions by the pressures of contemporary culture.

Discernment means that we teach our young people to "think Christianly," as Harry Blamires instructs in his classic *The Christian Mind.* Teenagers do not need to be taught to fear culture; they need to evaluate it according to the Scriptures and the standards of God. With sound teaching, young people can learn to discriminate between the good and the evil of our world, and then they can—with us—wrestle with the best means of communicating the Gospel to that world.

Such Christian thinking does not mean the removal of teenagers into Christian cloisters where they are taught to hold the darkness at bay. It means a courageous entrance into the world so that Christian truth can be addressed. This, according to Jacques Ellul, is the essence of Christian education (and therefore education within the home):

> Christian education must educate for risk and change. We must not shelter the young from the world's dangers, but arm them so that they will be able to overcome them. We are talking about arming them not with a legalistic or a moralistic breast-plate, but with the strength of freedom. We are teaching them not to fight in their own strength, but to ask for the Holy Spirit and to rely on Him. Parents must be willing to allow their children to be placed in danger, knowing that there is no possible education in Christ without the presence of real dangers in the world, for without danger, Christian education is only a worthless pretty picture which will not help at all when children first meet up with concrete life" (*Money and Power*, p. 123).

Educating with Christian values in the midst of the dangers of the world—this is the essence of discernment. Our goal must be to teach young people to see the truths and falsehoods of our culture with clarity so that they can walk the path that Jesus called "the narrow way" (see Matthew 7:14).

Your Own "Christian Critique"

In our youth group, we publish a monthly newsletter called the *Christian Critique*. In it we review movies, trends, current events, musicians, and songs that affect the lives of our teenagers. We discuss the issue at hand and then seek to evaluate it according to the Scriptures. The newsletter is not always easy to write because some of the issues of our world are decidedly gray with respect to right and wrong. Nevertheless, it is the ministry tool that has gotten the greatest amount of feedback from both parents and teenagers. Some are against it ("Christians should not even *think* of such things"), but most are enthusiastic about it because it helps them address the Christian faith to the modern world.

Perhaps what is needed are families who will get together for their own "Christian Critiques," teaching parents and children alike to ask questions of the media, advertising, and the culture-at-large. Then they can "have their senses exercised to discern both good and evil" (Heb. 5:14).

Why Convictions Must Be Consistent

Christian Chameleons

We live in a time of religious diversity and ethical neutrality. In the words of one of the Watergate perpetrators, we have lost our "moral compass," not just as individuals, but as a society. For this reason, one of the great challenges that a parent will face is the matter of building convictions into the teenager.

Like chameleons, we are all guilty of changing our colors according to our surroundings. The chameleon does this for self-protection; the more it disappears into the color of its environment, the less it is in danger from predators.

Unfortunately, the same is often true of us. We can modify our stands or our opinions according to the environment. In an age of religious pluralism and confused thinking, it is difficult to stand up and say that "no man comes to the Father" except through Jesus Christ. When marriage commitments are viewed as temporary and everyone seems to be having irreconcilable differences, how do we train our young people that God's design for marriage is lifelong?

Six Ways to Learn to Live by Convictions

If asked, "Would you like your teenager to grow to be a person who made a serious impact for the kingdom of God?" most Christian parents would respond with an emphatic "Yes!" The problem, however, is *how.*

As we look to the Scriptures to find examples of young men and women who made such an impact, we find that they were people of conviction. Their integrity set them apart from their peers and often apart from their culture. Joseph made great strides in pagan Egypt as a man of conviction. Daniel served under pagan kings, but he made them deal with the true God because of his life of conviction. Esther risked death to stand up for her people. Deborah obeyed the Lord and became a pillar of strength for Barak and all of Israel.

Assuming that we desire to build convictions into our teenagers, where do we begin? Again, there are no easy answers. The matter of living by convictions is a lifelong process, but there are some things that parents can do to start the building process.

1. *Personal example.* Virginia Brandt Berg once wrote that she'd rather "*see* a sermon than to hear one any day." Her words are a call for exemplary living, and it is a call that parents must heed. As a youth minister, I can say from much personal experience that the *example of the parents* is the single most important factor in building convictions into the life of the teenager.

In our efforts to disciple teenagers, we have had two

success routes. The first route is the teenager from the non-Christian family. For that young person, Christian commitment is in marked contrast to family standards, and Christian convictions are adopted as challenging and exciting.

The other success route (the majority of our so-called success cases) is with the teenager who has a committed Christian parent or parents. In this situation, the young person is excited about following Jesus Christ, and this excitement is manifested by imitation of the family member.

Jim had turned against the religion of his Christian parents at age fourteen. He figured that their deep commitment was excessive, and he wanted to have some fun rather than follow Jesus. Two years later, Jim committed himself to Christ on a youth retreat. The very next morning, Jim was up early reading the Bible. I asked him about this. He replied, "I really don't know what I am doing, but I know that I am supposed to get up every morning to read the Bible and pray. I know because I have seen Dad do it."

Jim was one day old as a Christian, but he already had a personal conviction about daily time for praying and Scripture reading. Why? Because he learned it from watching his father. And the conviction stuck. I followed Jim's track for five years after that weekend, and I never knew him to miss one day in reading and praying.

Tim Stafford emphasizes this point of personal example in the *Christianity Today* article quoted earlier:

Kids do not want to listen to reason or common sense. *The best witness from the adult world remains a life lived well,* with love and reverence for God and neighbor. That must make an impact, sooner or later (emphasis mine).

The best tool that the parent has to build convictions into the life of the teenager is his or her own life. Personal example is a teaching tool that teenagers can understand.

Amidst my rebellion during my teen years, my father and I frequently disagreed about morals, values, and life-styles. We argued about a lot of issues, but I never could criticize his personal consistency. He acted as he believed, and this, over the long haul, was the "life lived well" that I sought to imitate in faith and practice.

2. *Point them to the Bible.* An interview with several youth experts appeared in *Christianity Today* under the title, "The Myth of the Generation Gap" (October 19, 1984, pp. 14, 16). In it the experts revealed that there is some good news and some bad news about the convictions and values of the modern teenager.

The good news, according to the Reverend John Forliti, is that "parents are still of utmost importance to them [teenagers] in terms of values and beliefs. In fact, they outweigh peer influence." This is very good to hear, but there is also a negative side to consider.

According to Mark Wickstrom of Youth Leadership, Inc., religious education in the family is weak:

Few of them [teenagers] correlated biblical principles with the moral choices they made. Consistently they

78

made what looked like a Christian response, but when we asked about its base in the Bible, they didn't have the foggiest idea. They just thought it seemed Christian, or they'd vaguely heard that that was what Christians did.

These comments correlate with the findings of the "Religion in America" report of the Gallup/Associated Press Youth Survey (Gallup Report Number 222). In this study quoted in *Group* magazine, pollsters found that 95 percent of teenagers believe in God and that 90 percent of teenagers say that they pray. Yet of churched youths, only 3 percent can name all of the Ten Commandments; only 50 percent can name the four Gospels; and about 20 percent do not know the number of disciples that Jesus had! When we add to this the fact that 40 percent of these churched youths are involved in Bible-study groups, the reader wonders, "What happens at the Bible study?" (November/December, 1984, p. 27).

Faith without biblical basis. Beliefs without a scriptural foundation. If teenagers are to be people of conviction, then they must be pointed to the Scriptures, so that they are not dependent on family or church traditions as their only reason for belief.

Like the student, Jim, cited earlier, Glenn knew that being a Christian meant a daily time to meet with God. His family, however, emphasized the use of a devotional guide that scarcely mentioned more than one Bible verse. Glenn followed suit: his daily devotions became a verse, a story, a poem, and a prayer. His Christian commitment has seemed to last, but few of his friends would regard him as a man of conviction.

And the convictions he does have are based more on his family's beliefs than his knowledge of the Bible.

3. *Focus on the essential convictions.* There is a story about a Christian father and son in dialogue (the story may be true, or it may be apocryphal). The son came to his father to ask for permission to drive the car. His father responded, "Yes, under three conditions: first, you must clean up your room; second, you must read your Bible every day for the next month; and third, you must get a haircut" (the son's long hair was a frequent point of tension with the father).

A month went by, and the son appeared before the father. His room was spotless and he could document a month's reading in the Scriptures, but his hair was uncut. The son said, "Well, Dad, I have done what you asked. Now can I have the keys to the car?"

The father said, "I thought I told you that you had to get your hair cut first."

The son replied smugly, "Well, as I read the Gospels, I realized that Jesus had long hair, so I thought I should follow *Him*."

The father, not to be outdone, responded, "Yes, and Jesus *walked* wherever He went, and so will you."

This story offers a humorous look at this situation, but it is also a reflection of the way that parents can become preoccupied with trying to build nonessential convictions into teenagers. Is hair length really a theological issue, or does it just concern the father's preference? Should music or styles be such important issues to parents and teenagers?

There are some issues—issues that I consider peripheral—that can distract parents from emphasizing the basic foundational convictions of the Gospel.

Rock music is one example. There is no mention of it in the Scriptures, because it did not exist when the Bible was written. Lyrics are a legitimate concern, to be sure. (But so are the lyrics of country-western music, which often appeal to parents more than to teenagers. Remember, be consistent!) However, this issue is *not* the most important conviction of Christian faith.

I was saddened when a student in our group perceptively observed, "I think that my mother is more concerned about rock music than God is. She doesn't care if I hate my brothers, but she tells me that 'no good Christian listens to that kind of stuff.' I think her definition of being a Christian stinks."

Whatever the issue—movies, music, television, friends, dress—parents must first ask themselves this question: *Before I make a big issue out of _____, am I sure that my son/daughter understands the key issues of faith?*

It seems a shame when teenagers are crystal clear about why a Christian should never drink alcohol or should never dance, but they are incapable of explaining the plan of salvation to a friend. Somewhere along the line, somebody got priorities confused as to what the most important convictions really are!

4. *Hold them responsible for their choices.* One of the serious parent/teenager confrontations occurs when the teen makes active choices not to follow Jesus Christ. When it becomes evident that your teenager's "convictions" are more related to becoming successful or partying or achieving self-satisfaction than they are to following the Lord, then what?

Some parents go to extremes. On one extreme are

those who revert to the "if I ignore the problem, it will go away" attitude. They try to go through every day and week as if there is nothing wrong. Although they sense a deepening rift between themselves and the teenager, they refuse to acknowledge it (probably to avoid the pain). They overlook behaviors that are contrary to faith, and they prefer to maintain a "business as usual" attitude, even though the teenager has made some very important choices.

On the other extreme are those parents who perceive choices made by the teenager away from God as invitations to preach. Day in and day out, the rebel is reminded of the bad choices. Hell becomes the principal topic of discussion with respect to faith. Every day, the father or mother reminds the teenager, "I am praying for your salvation."

Neither extreme is correct. The first communicates to the teenager that the parents do not care about his or her decisions. The second forces the teenager to react to overbearing parents rather than consider a personal relationship with God.

The best option for parents is to communicate clearly the consequences of decisions to their young son or daughter. A reminder of the eternal nature of decisions toward or away from God is appropriate— but once or twice is enough. A clear set of life-style standards is also wise: "As long as you are in this house, you will join us in adhering to the following standards . . ."

Convictions are the beliefs we live by. If a teenager decides to live by beliefs that are contrary to Christian faith, the parents must allow the choice to be made (see the chapter on responsibility), but they must also be willing to let the teenager see that choices bring with them consequences—both short-term and long-term.

5. *Build their convictions about themselves.* In the lives of teenagers—especially those in early adolescence—the question of self-worth and personal identity is at the forefront of their psychological and emotional growth. Some misbehave to get attention and therefore prove to themselves that *I matter.* Others start to live out the result of a poorly formed self-image, and they react by getting angry, going to excesses in terms of personal appearance, or pushing themselves toward self-destruction (which can include drug abuse, eating disorders and, in its most extreme form, suicide).

One of the struggles that parents face in the teen years is the building of the child's self-esteem. Perhaps a father was too busy when the child was younger, and he never provided the needed attention. Now, the young teenager might have a poor sense of self-esteem. Perhaps mother, when she was younger, was struggling with her own sense of self-worth, so she overcompensated by verbally lashing her children. Now that these children are teenagers, they feel insecure about themselves, and they begin to make efforts at overcompensation.

Is there hope? Can healing take place? The good news is yes! Parents can still work hard to build a teenager's sense of self-worth, and this conviction can be cemented in the teenager's mind before he or she leaves home.

How? Here are a few suggestions based on the good

work I have observed in the parents who are making efforts in this area. First, remember that you and your teenager are different from each other. He needs to be allowed to behave as a teenager; she needs to be allowed to be silly, giggly, and starry-eyed about life. Parents who try to make a son or daughter a best friend can do great damage to the teenager. (This is especially dangerous in the single-parent situation; the parent may look at the teenager as a peer rather than a son or daughter.) The teenager needs to find a sense of self-worth as he is without being forced to be a miniature adult. Parents can enhance a teenager's self-esteem by allowing him to enjoy the process of growing up without rushing him into adulthood.

Another way that self-esteem is built as a conviction in the teenager is through affirmation. Fathers need to affirm their love verbally and physically—even to their sons! Ross Campbell *(How to Really Love Your Child)* and Gordon MacDonald *(The Effective Father)* have reminded parents of this strategic function of affirmation. Do not assume, *My son knows that I love him,* or *My daughter knows that I am proud of her.* They know these things only when you tell them, and failing to tell them could aggravate their sense of insignificance as people.

Some of my most awkward moments with my father occurred during my teens. He believed in telling me that he loved me, but I scarcely knew how to respond. Usually, a clumsy "Me, too," was all that I could muster. But my father never stopped telling me that he loved me. He knew—even before the books cited here were written—that a teenage son needs to know love from his dad, so he gave it.

6. *Give them the time and attention they need.* One person has put it this way: Teenagers do not understand "quality time"; they understand "quantity time." What this means is that teenagers may be more affected by parents spending a large block of time with them than by their having an "intense" hour of conversation. Young teenagers especially need to know that their lives are important enough to merit a mother's or a father's time. (*Note:* Quantity time is more effective in the life of the young teenager. Older teens who have started making their own schedules and have their own friends may find it difficult to spend a lot of time with Mom or Dad. By that time, a parent needs to concentrate on building self-worth through encouragement and other ways of showing interest in the son's or daughter's life.)

Success Story

Ken is one of the success stories of our youth group, and his success is largely a result of his devoted parents. They have built him in such a way that he has solid Christian convictions. He is an athlete in his public high school, yet he is unafraid to speak up about his faith, his stand on moral issues, and his choices in life. Ken tells his friends of his plans to be a missionary doctor, and he amazes his football buddies by telling them that losing his virginity is not on his list of things to do as he prepares for college next year.

Ken is a young man with convictions. He has grown through the example of consistent, Christian parents. He has learned how to research his own convictions from the Scriptures, and he has a deep desire to make changes in his world for the sake of Christ. On top of all this, Ken has a strong sense of self-worth. His parents have communicated their love for him, and he has known their support throughout junior and senior high school.

Ken is a testimony—not only to the Gospel—but also to the fact that the diligent efforts of parents can indeed build teenagers who live by convictions. Ken will probably make a powerful impact for Christ at college because his foundation is strong now. His parents built convictions into him through his teen years, and now they are seeing the positive results.

Why Sex and Morals Must Be Talked About Early

Frank Discussions a Must

Of all the subjects that I have been asked to address with parents of teenagers, none is more sensitive than that of sexual morality. Some parents are defensive, not wanting to hear what I have to say about sex and the American teenager. Others are beside themselves with worry, wondering how they can ever talk about the subject with their teenager.

Sexual activity is certainly part of the world of the teenager, and effective parenting requires that frank discussion take place between parent and teenager so that scriptural principles of being "above reproach" and biblical standards of morality can be clearly defined.

To exemplify the intensity of a parent-teen breakdown over moral failure on the part of the teenager, consider this letter to Ann Landers:

Dear Ann Landers:

Please do not congratulate me on becoming a grandfather. My daughter who had the baby is not married and you know it. The girl gave up her chance for an education, a good future, and the respect of her friends and relatives for a no-good bum.

The father of my grandchild dropped out of school in the 10th grade. He has no job and no ambition, nor is he interested in getting trained so that he can support himself, or the girl he made pregnant.

The only reason that I have permitted our daughter and her bastard brat to live under our roof is because my soft-hearted wife begged and pleaded with me not to throw them out on the street. I have no use for this weak, stupid girl who has denied me the joy of walking her down the aisle and giving her in marriage to a decent man I could be proud of.

To put it bluntly. Congratulations are not in order. Our daughter is a tramp.

Boston Globe, July 24, 1983

Harsh, hate-filled words by a man who is very bitter over the moral failure of his daughter—but one wonders if there is more to the story. Did the daughter understand sex? Was she using immorality as a means of demonstrating her anger toward her father? Under what conditions did she conceive? Had anyone taught her moral standards *before* it was too late?

Too often parents are more than willing to get angry over the sexual behavior of teenagers, but they are unwilling to discuss sex and morality with their son or daughter *before* problems occur. Thus, the teenager is often left to explore a sexual wilderness with the guidance of peers, romance novels, and sexual stereotypes portrayed in the media.

Effective relationships with teenagers require that parents be willing to undertake their responsibility to instruct teenagers about sexuality and moral standards.

Teaching Your Child about Sex

More than one parent has gotten sweaty palms and a nervous stomach over the prospect of talking to a son or daughter about sex. It is not easy for either party, so here are some basic principles that might ease the process.

Start early. After we showed one of the *Focus on the Family* films on adolescence, a father and his sixteen-year-old son returned home together. The father broke the silence in the car with a light-hearted, "Well, son, I guess it is about time that we had our little talk about the birds and the bees."

The son snapped back, "Okay, Dad, what is it that *you* wanted to know?"

The son was being sassy, but he made a good point. The average teenager, by age sixteen, has already gotten a thorough (although not always accurate) schooling about sex. If the teen has not learned it from Mom or Dad, then peers, books, television, the movies, and locker-room jokes have been sources of such information.

Talking with your child about sex should probably occur before the teen years are in full swing. It is best to start the conversations before puberty has started.

Dr. James Dobson has some very helpful insights on this conversation process in his book *Preparing For Adolescence*, and I highly recommend it as reading for parents of preteens.

If your teenager is already fourteen, fifteen, or older, and you have never had a conversation about sex, all is not lost. Start where you are, and use some of the other principles discussed here.

Take responsibility. In one school system, parents of junior highers were irate about the offering of sex education classes in the physical education curriculum. They were offended because they had not been asked for their permission; they were upset because they thought that sexual mechanics were being taught without the assignment of moral or ethical values; and they were indignant because "After all, such education is the responsibility of the parents in the home!"

The parents won their case, and perhaps they are right. Perhaps the junior high Physical Education 100 class is not the place for sex education. But I wonder if such education is really happening at home. I wonder how many parents *are* taking responsibility for the education of teenagers concerning the physiological, moral, and even spiritual dimensions of sex.

Good moral education can occur only when parents take the responsibility upon themselves. Good parenting means that parents of teenagers and preteens see themselves as the God-ordained teachers of their children with respect to sexuality.

Talk honestly. After another of the *Focus on the Family* films, a single mother and her thirteen-year-old son returned home. In the film, Dr. Dobson had spent a large amount of time discussing masturbation. The mother thought to herself as she drove, *Whew, I am so glad that Jim Dobson addressed that subject in his film. I do not know how I would have brought it up otherwise.*

When they got into the house, they sat in the kitchen for some milk and cookies. The mother gingerly directed the conversation to the film. "What did you think?" she asked.

"Not much," replied her son, "except I have this one question."

"What's that?" asked the mom, not knowing what was coming.

"What's masturbation?"

The mother had thought that she had been absolved of the tough conversation because Dr. Dobson had addressed it for her. The only problem was that her thirteen-year-old did not know what the film was talking about. He probably knew what masturbation was; he just did not know it by that name.

Talking with your teenager about sex does not mean giving a lecture out of a physiology textbook. It means talking in terms that the teenager understands. It may mean saying things such as, "This is the scientific term, but you might hear it referred to at school as _____ ." If the parent does not talk in terms that are familiar to the teenager, the conversation is fruitless.

Honest conversation between parent and teenager can include some embarrassing moments for the mother or father (like that of the single mother described here). It can mean a frank discussion of commitment to Jesus (like telling your teenage son,

"There will be times when the only thing that can keep you out of bed is your commitment to Jesus Christ"). It can result in increased communication between parent and teenager because the teenager feels more confident in bringing questions about sex and morality to Mom or Dad.

Engage in discussions, not lectures. One father in our church saved himself a lot of grief by involving his son in a discussion about sex. His son was then ten, and the father decided that it was about time to have a talk on "where babies come from" with the boy. The father expounded accurately and thoroughly on the process of reproduction, and then he described the act of sexual intercourse. Up until that point, it was a lecture. Then the father opened it up for questions.

The only question the ten-year-old son had concerning sexual intercourse: "*Why* would anyone want to do that?"

At this point, the father realized that enough had been said for one evening. He did not want to get too far ahead of his son.

One danger of the subject of sex and morality is that parents can hide their nervousness and personal insecurity by turning a friendly talk into a judgmental-sounding lecture. Questions from the teenager can result in harsh responses that stem from fear that the teenager might have already experimented with sex. Such responses will virtually eliminate the likelihood of future conversations about the subject.

The writers of *The Private Life of the American Teenager* offer this advice:

You're more likely to strike a responsive chord by discussion and reasoning than by unyielding rule-setting. If you fear, for example, that your daughter will be sexually exploited and abused by an older and more experienced new boyfriend, discuss the situation with her and offer her your knowledge. . . . In contrast, if you simply forbid the relationship, you have lost the opportunity to convey your viewpoint or discuss any questions she might have about the relationship (p. 157).

Listening, responding, and discussing will usually yield much greater results than one-sided lectures. Teenagers will have questions. Some will be like those you had as a teenager. Others will be new to you, so you must listen and respond with compassion, conviction, and correct answers.

Seek to understand their world. The parent who glibly remarks, "The sex scene in high school is the same as it was in my day," has not done much research. The world today is different from the world of twenty or thirty years ago. Teenagers now are faced with decisions about virginity and "how far is too far?" and they are also faced with questions of sexual preference: "Am I gay? Can a Christian be a homosexual?"

Many of the issues of sex are the same as they have always been, but the teenagers are faced with these issues *earlier* than before. Junior highers wonder about virginity. Unwanted pregnancies are too-frequent occurrences with thirteen- and fourteen-year-old girls.

Add to these realities the stereotypes of sex and morality presented in the media. A husband or wife is scarcely ever presented as being faithful to a spouse. A dating relationship always includes scenes in the bedroom. The images of sex and sex-in-relationships that fill the teenage mind are usually far from biblical standards and sometimes equally as far from reality in our world.

To be effective in discussing sexual decisions and the matters of moral choices, parents must know where their teenagers are coming from. Knowing this will help you understand their questions, and it will help you present answers that are relevant to their situations.

Set a good example. The matter of consistency is critical because teenagers have a great ability to point out hypocrisy. If a father tells his son that a Christian is one who keeps his sexual appetites under control—yet that father is obese—the son might easily reason, "Well, why don't you keep *your* appetites under control?"

In another situation, the mother or father who watches soap operas or reads immoral novels is saying, in effect, to the son or daughter, "You cannot commit adultery or fornication, but it is okay to watch or read about people who do."

Parents who desire to build strong moral convictions and sexual control in teenagers must first set the pace themselves. There is no room for the "Do as I say, not as I do" attitude.

Setting a good example also includes the parent's conveyance of a proper attitude toward sex. Teenagers who gain a "sex is dirty" or "sex is sin" attitude from their parents will have great difficulty in their perspectives. Not only will they grow up with an unhealthy view of sex, they are likely to carry that view into marriage.

Parents are wise to teach teenagers that sex is great and beautiful and a gift from God—provided it is kept in the proper context of marriage. The biblical writers often made sexual love analogous to fire. Like fire, sex is wonderful when contained in its proper context, but when it is out of control, it results in destruction.

Qualities Related to Sexual Morality

Other qualities discussed in this book are related to this subject of sexual morality. *Forgiveness* may be required for the teenager who has already failed. *Honesty* is certainly a requirement in conversations about the subject. *Discernment* is a necessity for the ability to see good from evil.

The healthy parent-teen relationship does not assume that teenagers have all the answers about sexuality. Nor does it take for granted that teenagers will make the right choices without instruction and example. Instead, the healthy relationship tackles the issue head-on so that both parent and teenager can grow.

Why Teenagers Need Freedom to Fail

A Different World

If one observes the world of animals, it is easy to see a rather perfunctory process of parenting. The baby is born; the maturation process is accelerated; and in a very short time, the offspring is thoroughly independent to hunt, breed, and exist on its own.

The process of taking a child from birth to adult independence is not nearly so rapid or complete as it seems to be among animals. Interdependence is life-long, and maturity stages are somewhat unpredictable.

We touched on the basic problem of adolescence in the chapter on *responsibility* (Chapter 3). Teenagers are both children and adults, and yet, in another way, they are neither. They exist in a kind of limbo, where there is no sense of "place."

The long process of human maturation, combined with the extended period of adolescence, leads to some serious problems with respect to freedom. Should teens be pushed out of the nest when parents are wary about their ability to fly? How much leverage should they be given when it comes to making decisions about their own lives?

How Much and How Soon?

Freedom—how much should my teenager be given? And how soon? How do I know if he or she is ready to act responsibly?

A study published in the annual edition of *Today's Education* revealed how teenagers spend their money. Twenty-six million teenagers spent $45 billion in one year. How did they spend this money? The top items were records, gasoline, cosmetics, clothing, entertainment, hobbies, and snacks (statistics from *Sources and Resources*, January, 1985). Most parents would look at that result and say, "See! It just reveals how unprepared teenagers are to handle their lives. Freedom? Forget it!"

Peter's parents did not want him to have freedom. Until he was eighteen, they made almost every important decision for him. They kept him rather sheltered from his high school world, and they refused to let him have many friends. They bought his clothes, dropped him off at and picked him up from school, and welcomed him into their social sphere (so that he would not hang around with teenagers).

Then Peter went to college. He became irresponsible, sloppy, and very nervous. He came home every weekend, retreated to the family room, and watched television. He could not cope, and at age twenty, he had a nervous breakdown and dropped out of college.

Now, at age thirty-one, Peter lives with his aging parents and holds down a minimum-wage job.

Peter is an extreme case, to be sure, but he is a composite of all of the worst things that can happen to those who never break free from parents. They are not equipped to face the real world, and when they are finally thrust into adult responsibility, they retreat to a fantasy world (which is as secure as the world they knew as teenagers) or they crumble under the pressure.

Parents need to work hard to give children freedom, even before the teenage years. The basic function of parenting is to raise a son or daughter to be independent and able to cope as an adult. Giving freedom is a requirement for growth.

The Types of Freedom

Freedom and *responsibility* (Chapter 3) must go hand in hand, but freedom has a sense of letting children go without providing a safety net. It means pushing them out of the nest progressively until they can fly alone.

What types of freedom? Consider these three:

1. *Freedom to fail.* This subject is referred to under the topics of *responsibility* and *forgiveness,* but it bears mentioning once again. Growth and maturity can only occur in the life of the teenager when parents give the freedom to make mistakes, bad choices, and errors in judgment.

Dr. David Elkind once again speaks to this issue:

Although this may seem hard-hearted, it [letting them fail] has the greatest benefit for the teenager and for us. If we make a habit of taking on the teenager's responsibilities because we dislike the consequences of failure for him or her, we deprive the young person of a crucial experience of becoming an adult. The consequences of failure are more severe for adults, and we should not set up our youngsters for painful lessons they could have learned in the early years with little trouble (p. 212).

Mrs. Edwards desperately wanted her daughter, Michelle, to look good in my eyes. She was pushing Michelle to apply for one of our youth summer-mission trips, although Michelle seemed apathetic about it. When it appeared that Michelle was going to miss the deadline, her application form arrived in the mail. It was typed neatly, and it was articulate—the opposite of the qualities in Michelle's life at that point. I flipped it over to look at the signature; then I researched her registration card for Sunday school.

It did not take too much detective work to conclude that the application had come from Mrs. Edwards, not her daughter. Mrs. Edwards had panicked and covered up for Michelle's slovenly behavior.

I finally got the courage to talk to Mrs. Edwards. My basic question was this: "Who will cover for Michelle in three years when she is in college and her papers are due?"

I must confess that my parents (especially my father) found it difficult to allow me to fail. Although I was almost always an *A* student, my only memory of his evaluation of my report card was when I got less than *A*'s. "Why aren't these *B*'s *A*'s?" he would ask, and I would shrink away with feelings of failure.

Whatever caused him to be intolerant of failure in me carried into my life as well, illustrating that my adult maturation was affected by his unwillingness to give me freedom to fail.

Giving teenagers freedom to fail is tough on parents, especially if the success means more to the parent than it does to the young person. (If you do not believe me, watch some fathers and mothers yell and scream at their teenagers' athletic events—it really makes you wonder whose success or failure is at stake.)

When a young person fails, the self-involved parent wants to look for excuses because he or she desires either to protect the teenager or to protect himself or herself from the pain that failure brings. Such excusing, however, is extremely hazardous for the growth process. Listen to Dr. Elkind again:

> It would be wrong, a serious mistake, I believe, to excuse any and all teenage misbehavior as a consequence of bad social upbringing and social upheaval. These factors are important, particularly today, but at some point teenagers must be held accountable for their own actions (p. 80).

Fred Donald simply could not accept the fact that his son, Art, was a poor student. For three years of high school, Fred blamed everyone. He found fault with the school system, the principal, the elementary-school-reading program, and even the school counselor. Finally, Art's grades were so poor that Fred put his son into prep school. There, Art squeaked by, and he barely got into a junior college. Now, Art is struggling again. His grades are poor, and his morale is low. Fred is starting to blame teachers and curriculum, but it is almost as if Art knows the truth: He is not a high performance student. I wonder to myself how long Fred will keep blaming others before he can allow Art to do his best at the level of his abilities.

2. *Freedom to have "space."* Secrets usually drive parents crazy. On a Saturday morning, if a mother sees her daughter writing in a little book, she might ask, "What's that you are writing in?"

"My diary," replies the thirteen-year-old daughter.

"What are you writing about?" asks Mom.

"Oh, nothing." The daughter wraps up her entry, closes the book, and leaves the room. She can see that she will not get much written with a nosy mother around.

After such an incident, the mother could do one of three things. She could write it off as a cute, teenage action (that she herself had done). She could start to worry, *What is she writing in that thing?* (remembering the things that *she* wrote in *her* diary). Or she could start scheming about how she could get to read that diary.

One of the painful aspects of teenage maturation for parents is the realization that their children are growing up. The children are not telling the parents everything anymore. They are starting to have secrets. When this realization strikes, parents have to make an active decision to accept the fact that a personal sense of identity *away from* the parent is a healthy sign of growth in the teenager.

Where do teenagers desire this space? I did a little informal survey of our teenagers through asking questions about freedom. I inquired about the actions their parents took that drove them crazy, and I asked in what areas of their lives they wanted space. Here are some of their responses:

"I hate it when my parents barge into my room without knocking or asking permission. They would be furious if I did that to them."

"My mother opens my mail—even the stuff from the church. I guess it really doesn't bother me too much, but then again, I never really have gotten any mail that I do not want her to see."

"The other day, after school, I came home early and my mother was in my room. She said that she was dusting, but I could tell that she had been going through my drawers. Why can't she let me have something to myself?"

"One Saturday, my father was throwing things out of the attic, and he had a box of my junior high stuff. He figured that—now that I was a high school senior—I wouldn't want it anymore. I got really mad, because these things are *my* memories, and I wish he would mind his own business."

"My mother and father have no regard for my time or my freedom. Every time I decide to stay home, they make me the baby-sitter for my two little sisters (who are truly a pain!), and I don't get paid or anything. They must think it's great to have me as their slave."

"Every time I talk to my boyfriend on the phone, I swear that my father is listening in. Sometimes I want to say something really bad just to get a reaction out of him."

These findings are also confirmed in *The Private Life of the American Teenager,* pp. 30–36.

Usually, teenagers do not expect total independence from parents. They only desire to be allowed the freedom to have some things to themselves. Their mail, rooms, records, diaries, memories, friends, and phone calls are precious to them, and they expect their parents to let them keep these private.

There are obvious cases in which such freedom should be exempted (such as reading the diary of a teenager who seems dangerously suicidal), but these cases are rare in most families. The better solution— if there is something suspicious going on—is to talk first. Ask questions as an expression of your desire to respect the teen's freedoms and space. Then, if you are still not satisfied that the truth is being told, forewarn of a raid or search. Yes, there may still be time for the teenager to cover up, but even this is not as damaging as the long-term breakdown in trust that occurs when a teenager's personal belongings are scrutinized without warning.

3. *Freedom from embarrassment.* It is easy for parents to maintain the opinion that the real world is an adult world and that teenagers need to fit in. This attitude, however, negates the fact that teenagers have feelings and ideas to be considered, especially in public situations.

Again, hearing from teenagers gives parents the best ideas of what behaviors should be avoided so as to give their teenagers minimum feelings of embarrassment or humiliation. Here are the seven points they would tell parents to avoid embarrassing them (also confirmed in *The Private Life of the American Teenager*):

- "Do not reprimand me in front of my friends."

- "Don't criticize or praise me in front of *your* friends."

- "Don't make 'scenes' in public."

- "Don't treat me like a baby."

- "When my friends are around, do not pry into their lives."

- "Please avoid affection in public places."

- "In front of my friends, please don't act stupid."

Sound familiar? Of course, these are some distinctly teenage expectations, but they do teach parents something about allowing teenagers freedom to be themselves. It also reminds parents of how important it is to most teenagers to give a positive impression to their friends.

I respect Mr. and Mrs. Kenyon for their willingness to give their teenage daughter, May, freedom from embarrassment. The Kenyons are extremely effective in counseling teenagers, so I asked them if they would serve as teachers in our high school Sunday-school class. They promised to think and pray about it.

They returned with their answer: *no.* I wondered why.

"When we asked May, she gave it some thought too, and then she said, 'I love you, Mom and Dad, but if you join the high school group, *it will really cramp my style.'* So we think we are wisest to let her see the high school group as her own, not something she has to share with us."

Freedom—To What Degree?

The question of how much freedom obviously has to be modified for each teenager. Some will be more prepared or desirous of freedom than others. Consider these factors when deciding just how much freedom might be appropriate:

Age. Growth is progressive. An eighteen-year-old needs more freedom than a fourteen-year-old. Each parent must decide how much freedom can be given at what age. The goal should be to help teenagers grow—not to overwhelm them with more freedom than they can manage.

Some parents allow teenagers to start dating in junior high school. Others set the magic age of sixteen. Still others wait until the dating opportunity arises, and they pass judgment based on the person being dated and the type of date.

Gender. In general (and I am fully aware of how dangerous it is to generalize about teenagers), teenage girls are more mature and capable of handling freedom than teenage boys. In general, girls are also more self-conscious, more aware of their need for space, and more likely to be embarrassed by their parents.

Remember the case of May Kenyon? Having her parents around in the youth group would cramp her style. An identical situation arose with Mike and Shawn, whose parents were considering youth work in our group. When they were asked, these teenage boys replied, "Sure, we would like to have them around; it wouldn't bother us at all."

Freedom must be conditioned according to both the need for space and the maturity level of the teenager, and the difference between young men and young women can certainly be a factor in this respect.

Experience. Perhaps as you read this book, you think, *I have never given my teenager responsibility or freedom. Now where do I start?*

Obviously, freedom should not be dumped on a teenager who is unprepared and ill-equipped to manage it. There must be adjustments according to proven experience and responsible behavior. The best way to decide is to give gradual amounts of freedom at a time, so as to see the teen's ability to deal with it.

As has been stated throughout this book, *the best solution is to know your teenager.* Understanding his or her growth and maturity level is the best way to respond with appropriate amounts of freedom.

School environment. Although parents should not succumb to peer pressure, they should temper their dispersement of freedom according to the environment of the teenager's school. For example, if you are in a community in which many teenagers marry after high school graduation, forbidding your teenager to date until age sixteen may be unrealistic.

The high school environment can play a positive role. In the Lexington (Massachusetts) school system, high schoolers are very studious and hard working. To get along with their peers, high schoolers must study. Therefore, parents can give teenagers more freedom with respect to their time because they know that the school environment will encourage teenagers to be responsible in their use of it.

The school environment will put pressure on teenagers in a variety of directions. If most teens have cars, then parents may need to give freedom in the realm of learning to drive and being responsible for a car. If most high schoolers return from school when neither parent is home, parents who have decided to have someone at home after school may find their teenager desirous of more free time.

The goal is *not* conformity to the community or to the school system, however. The goal is to understand the world that the teenager comes out of so that you, the parent, can more appropriately respond in the delegation of freedom.

Motivation. The final factor to consider when giving freedom is the matter of motivation. Ask yourself: *How badly does my teenager want freedom?* There are two points to keep in mind. First, *be cautious about the lethargic teenager who desires no freedom.* Remember the case of Peter at the beginning of this chapter? He did not want freedom. He liked being in the security of an overprotective home.

When a parent perceives that the teenager is unwilling to undertake personal freedoms, there is reason for concern. Some will respond to gentle "nudges," and they will rise to the occasion when freedoms are given. Others, however, who demonstrate a chronic lack of desire may be manifesting some warning signals of severe depression (or even suicidal thoughts) that warrant a visit to a professional adolescent counselor or the counselor at school.

A second matter to keep in mind is that *there will be some teenagers who are overly zealous for freedom.* This teen will want to drive at age thirteen, start a realty company at age fifteen, and run for president before graduating from high school! The craft for the parent here is to delegate freedoms and responsibilities without overdoing it. The zeal must not be crushed, but on the other hand, there must be an element of caution so that the teenager does not get set up for a devastating failure—one that could turn that zeal into apathy.

Most teenagers will fall somewhere in between these two extremes with respect to motivation. The most important thought for parents to remember is that freedoms need to be *gradually* given so that—by age eighteen or so—the teenager will be as prepared as possible to start handling full adult freedoms and independence.

Why Trust Is Hard to Accomplish

Mixed Feelings

At age seventeen, I became a Christian. After five years of bluffing God and my parents, I came to a point of repentance and a new start.

As part of my "new life" in Christ, I sensed the need to ask my parents' forgiveness for all of the lies and deceit I had perpetrated in the previous years. I sat down with them and revealed what I had *really* been doing for five years.

Although I was sharing out of a genuine desire to testify to the change that God had made in my life, my parents were less than overjoyed. I am sure they were thinking, *When did he do this?* or *How did he get away with that?* or *Should we ever believe anything he tells us in the future?*

For me, it was a testimony of God at work in my life. For my parents, however, the spiritual blessing was

111

overshadowed by the feelings of being betrayed or duped for the five previous years. They had to wonder if they could ever trust me again.

The Tough Question

"But you don't trust me, do you?"

When a teenager asks for privileges and the parent assigns conditions to the privileges, the natural response of the young person is "Why? Don't you trust me?"

When this question arises, a parent is put into a position in which no answer will suffice. If the parent responds, "Yes, of course I trust you," then the teenager will ask, "Then why these conditions?"

If the parent, on the other hand, responds, "No, I do not trust you," then the teenager will pour on the guilt, "Oh, great relationship we have here; my parents don't even trust me!"

Trust: confidence, faith, belief in someone's goodness or integrity. Reading a definition like this will cause most parents to roll their eyes and wonder out loud, "How can I *ever* trust my teenager? Everything he does tells me that he is not reliable and that I should *not* trust him."

Indeed, building a relationship with a teenager by trusting him is a monumental task. Yet it must be done. The qualities that have been covered in past chapters all require a level of trust in the interaction of parent and teenager. Trust must be built into the relationship to enable the teenager to grow toward mature adulthood.

What Trust Is Not

Before proceeding to discussions about what this trust is and how it can be built in the family relationship, we must first focus on what trust is *not.*

First, trust is not a belief in your teenager's inherent goodness. Only a fool would try to believe this. The "free-form" parenting style of some, which allows rebellion to manifest itself because "the teenager must be allowed freedom of self-expression," denies the reality of sin. You should not put your trust in your teenager just because he or she is growing into adulthood. (I know many adults who should not be trusted and so do you.) Whatever trust is given must be given with a full knowledge of a teenager's sinfulness. "Foolishness is bound up in the heart of a child" (Prov. 22:15) the Bible states, and the parent should not try to defy this truth by an unconditional trust in the teenager.

Second, trust is not unmerited confidence. An element of proven experience is necessary to build trust between parent and teenager. If a young person squanders money every time he receives it, it is senseless to trust him again if there have been no corrective measures taken to make him more responsible and trustworthy.

Finally, trust is not blind faith. Some parents prefer to overlook the failures of teenagers. When a teenager is told to be home by 11:00 P.M., and she arrives at 12:30 A.M., she should be confronted. The parent who stays away from the confrontation thinking, *But I don't want her to think that I don't trust her,* makes a mistake that will break down the parent/teen relationship, not build it.

113

What Trust Is

Having examined what trust is *not*, we must ask the question: What *is* this trust? or, more specifically, What is the trust needed to improve relationships within the home? There are two levels of trust needed in the interaction of parent and teenager that can be built to improve rapport and communication: (1) *trust in your teenager;* and (2) *trust in God.*

To be effective as parents requires a growing ability to trust your teens (and to trust the work that you have already put into them). This, however, does not happen in an isolated relationship; the power of God and trust in Him can enable parents to grow.

Let's explore how to build each level of trust.

How to Build Trust in Your Teen

Although there is an element of trust that must be *given*, much trust (at least in the parent/teen relationship) is earned or built. Trust given as a result of love (remember 1 Cor. 13:7: "Love . . . bears all things, believes [or trusts] all things, hopes all things, endures all things"?) must be offered as a gift. Trust that is built, however, can be enhanced by a parent if several principles are incorporated into the parent/teen relationship:

1. *Have clearly stated guidelines and rules.* Much of the breakdown in trust occurs because the parent assumes the mature response of the teenager. When the parent tries to rebuke the teen for an offense, he or she might reply, "But I never knew . . ." A parent can help

alleviate this problem by having clearly stated rules about curfews, volume of the stereo, behavior in the home, and so on.

Most teenagers I know are not inherently wise, and when they fail or misbehave, parents often respond with a hopeless "How can I ever trust you when you do things like that?" Such despair need not be present for the parent who is willing to anticipate the problem areas and set clear guidelines *before* a crisis occurs, thus helping the teenager to be more trustworthy.

Setting these guidelines can be taken to an extreme, however, and no parent should take this advice for a license to set up a totalitarian regime in which there is a rule for everything. One approach would be for the parent to decide the ten most important issues on which the teen needs guidelines or rules. This limits the rule making, but it still offers the teenager clearly stated mandates for behavior in the most critical areas (language, dress, music, and so forth).

What happens when the teenager obviously blows it, and there is no stated rule? Every situation must be handled individually. There may be times when the parent needs to say, "All right; I did not tell you to be home by 10:00 P.M., so you are not in trouble. But in the future, let's be clear—10:00 P.M. is the curfew unless we agree differently."

In other situations (using vulgar language, stealing, or responding with physical violence), the parent has to punish, even if there were no stated rules known to the teenager. Someone has said that "ignorance of the law is no excuse," and this adage must be applied at home at times.

2. *Reward trust that has been kept.* Many teenagers become frustrated in family situations in which good behavior is ignored and bad behavior is carefully scrutinized. Too many parents fail to affirm teenagers when they behave well or when they keep the rules. Thus, when they punish teenagers for the one time they break the rules, the teenagers respond with anger or frustration: "How come you never notice when I do things *right?*"

Terry is a trustworthy teenager, and I am happy to give her responsibility in our youth group. Her trustworthiness has been built at home. Her parents made an active choice to set clear guidelines for responsible behavior. When Terry fulfilled these guidelines, her parents affirmed her and praised her behavior. Soon, Terry loved doing the right things because they created peace and happiness at home, something that teenagers appreciate and need. Now—in a context outside the home—she knows how to be trustworthy and to follow directions because her parents built these things into her through their encouragement.

Psychologists call this "positive reinforcement," and it is effective. Rewarding good behavior has much better effects on relationships than punishing bad behavior. Basically, this means that parents should make efforts to thank teenagers for keeping the rules. I apply this principle in my youth group. When students are well behaved and obedient, I thank them and tell them that their good actions make it much easier for me to trust them.

3. *Be trustworthy.* The parent who is in the habit of failing to fulfill promises to the teenager is asking for trouble. The teenager follows the example that is set, and if the parent is not trustworthy, the teen will tend to follow that example.

Ben is a businessman who travels quite often. He frequently tells fourteen-year-old Ben, Jr., that he will come to his basketball games, but he never seems to make it. Something always comes up, or an unexpected business trip gets planned, and Ben fails to make it to the games. Over the period of a year, the relationship between father and son breaks down, so Ben comes to me with this question: "Why are we growing so far apart?"

My answer is simple. Ben, Jr., no longer trusts his father. His father has shown himself to be a man who can't be counted on to keep his word, so the son puts distance between them. Soon—if Ben, Jr., is a normal teenager—he will begin to act the same way. He will begin to hurt his father intentionally because he is treating his father as he has been treated. If Ben wants the relationship to be restored, he had better start being a man of his word to his son. Trustworthiness begets trustworthiness.

4. *Forgive.* In all relationships, trust is violated because we are sinners. The interaction of parent and teenager is no exception. Your young person will make mistakes. It is at this point that the grace of God comes into play, giving the parent the ability to forgive and to restate trust in the teenager by offering a second chance.

When a teenager violates a trust, the parental response of "I will never let you do that again" seldom yields good results. Forgiveness through the power of

Jesus Christ will allow the parent to say instead, "Yes, you blew it. I forgive you, though, and I will trust you again."

On a missions trip with thirteen members of our youth group, I had the opportunity of being in the parental position of giving trust. One of the older teenagers, Dave, age eighteen, was put in charge of six of his peers as they shopped in a foreign city.

Following my own advice, I told him the exact guidelines, "Don't let the group split up, and be back to the hotel by 6:00 P.M."

At 6:00 P.M., the group was there, and I thanked Dave for his good job (rewarding a trust that had been kept). The group, however, seemed shaken. When I inquired, I found that Dave had let the group get split up, and they had spent the majority of the afternoon trying to find one another.

I confronted Dave; he told me the whole story and asked forgiveness for his mistake. I forgave him, and I told him that he would be in charge of the same group the next day. Although he had failed, I wanted him to know that I would trust him again. Dave came through with flying colors the next day. He proved himself trustworthy as a leader.

How to Build Trust in God

Christian parents do not build trust only in teenagers. Bringing this issue of trust to the faithful God will add perspective and hope to the parent/teen relationship. The issue of trusting teenagers is actually secondary. The primary issue is this: *Can God be trusted with our teenagers to bring them through to re-*

sponsible adulthood and mature Christian life-style?

Although most Christian parents respond with an emphatic *yes,* their behavior (and worries and anxieties) often reveal their true fears. In a world of alternative life-style choices, pornographic literature, flexible moral standards, and questionable ethics, most parents are quite fearful about their teenagers. Their uneasiness reveals a shallowness in their ability to trust God.

There are several principles parents can put into practice that will help them build their trust in God concerning teenagers:

1. *Remember the past.* In the Scriptures, the people of faith are exhorted to remember God's works of the past to build their faith for the present. To recall that God brought them forth from Egypt would help the Israelites face new challenges. To remember that God raised Jesus from the dead would bring faith to persecuted apostles.

Parents must remember the past if they are to trust God about the present and the future of teenagers. Remembering how God delivered them from turbulent teen years can give parents faith to believe that God can do the same in their teenagers. Remembering that the teenagers as infants were dedicated to the Lord reminds parents of the One who is ultimately in charge.

2. *Go to the Bible and to prayer.* At every crisis point of life, we need to get perspective, and God's perspective comes through quiet moments of listening to His Word and of getting His mind in prayer. There is a subtle tendency in parents to look for some magical

solution to raising teenagers. Unfortunately, some spend much more time worrying or looking for the instant solution than they spend seeking God's will. Perhaps this is why trust in God is lacking.

To build trust in God, read His Word. Focus on His promises. Trust the truths put forth in Scripture. In prayer, bring your concerns about your teenager before God. He knows. He cares about the fear and pain and confusion that many parents of teenagers are going through.

Going to God's Word and to prayer may not produce instant results, but it can produce trust. It can reassure the fearful parent that God is mighty enough to handle every crisis. It can quiet the anxious parent who wonders what will ever become of a rebellious teenager.

Going to God's Word and to prayer helps parents of teenagers gain God's perspective. *He* is still in charge!

In my case, my parents were able to rebound from the ill effects of my testimony to be able to trust me again. They could do this because they were people of prayer, and they knew that God had been faithful to bring me to Him. The route that God chose was not the easiest for them, but they trusted in Him.

3. *Look to other parents.* Many parents of teenagers (like teenagers themselves) suffer from an "I'm the only one who ever went through this" syndrome. Feelings of failure and loneliness plague many parents, yet they are afraid to speak of these feelings because they think no one will understand.

Other parents of teenagers can be God-given assets to the church or community in terms of learning to trust God. The cooperative venture of parents working together adds perspective *(Maybe things are not as bad as I thought)* and wisdom *(Mrs. Jones handled this situation in this way; maybe I should too).*

Building trust in God does not just happen in the quiet moments of personal devotion. It also occurs through the voices of other people who speak of how God worked in their situations. "In the multitude of counselors there is safety" (Prov. 11:14). Parents of teenagers need to be resources to one another so that they can counsel and console one another.

Do you want to learn to trust God with your teenagers? Then perhaps you should get together with some other parents and learn together how to support one another and build one another's faith in the challenging task of parenting teenagers.

Trust. It is a *gift;* it is *earned.* We can learn to trust others, and we can build trust into our relationships. For the parents who desire to build trust between themselves and their teenagers, and for the parents who aspire to trust God with their teenagers, there is a way. Trust can be built if parents are willing to dedicate the time and effort needed.

Why Teenagers— and Parents— Need Forgiveness

Ineffective Responses

The Beatles produced a song some years ago entitled "She's Leaving Home." In it, the parents of a young woman (probably a teenager) awaken to find that their daughter has run away. Their responses differ. The father seems apathetic; the mother focuses on her own hurt: She dwells on the pain her daughter has caused her and the embarrassment she will cause with her friends.

There is a depth of pain possible in the relationship of parent and teenager that is difficult to explain to an outside observer. Harsh words (from a teenager who is starting to learn the power of the tongue) can wound a parent deeply. On the other hand, bitter or violent responses from a parent can create a chasm in the relationship that can never be bridged.

The parents in the Beatles' song illustrate the two most ineffective responses to the rebellion of teenagers. The first is apathy, most often present in the parent who is tired of putting up with the hassle. The father's apathy says, in effect, "Let her go; she was only causing trouble here anyhow. Maybe now we can find some peace."

The second is the self-centered response: "How could she do this to *me?*" This is the response of the parent who is more concerned for personal feelings ("How could my kid hurt me so much?") or for personal reputation ("What will they say at church when they find out?") than for the teen involved.

My purpose in this closing chapter is not to justify the unreasonable or rebellious behavior of teenagers. Nor is it to tell parents that their feelings do not matter and that they should bend over backwards to accommodate the unruly actions of a son or daughter. The purpose is to set forth one basic premise: Healthy relationships within the home between parent and teenager require the *quality of forgiveness*.

To put it another way, relationships will thrive at home when the parent and the teenager accept the fact that each must treat the other as he or she *needs* to be treated, not as he or she *deserves* to be treated. In short, relationships in the home need mercy.

The Why of Forgiveness

This is one question that is easy to answer. Mercy and forgiveness are needed because people sin. *Teenagers sin. Parents sin.* "There is none righteous, no, not one" (Rom. 3:10).

Few parents need convincing about a teenager's sinfulness. The mischievousness of the teen years often produces deceitfulness, vandalism, or experimentation with drugs or alcohol. On the relational side, the teenage years bring forth a spirit of independence that can wrongly manifest itself in a sassy tongue or a belligerent attitude toward parents.

What parents do need to recognize, however, is that teenagers sin for a variety of reasons. Some are simply ignorant and curious about life. Other are genuinely rebellious and try to hurt others. Some enjoy their sins and will not be deterred by a glib rebuke that "only God's ways lead to happiness." Others simply show that they lack judgment and the ability to think and live according to long-term values. The parents who recognize why teenagers sin will be better able to respond.

There is a second reason why forgiveness is a must for good rapport at home: *parents sin*. Those who are put in God-given positions of authority and leadership still sin; they blow it. Whenever the topic is sin, there is always a tendency to want to focus on the sins of the other. Parents want to focus on the teenager's sins rather than remember that they sin too.

In thinking about this topic of forgiveness, parents need to recognize their own sinfulness because they will not be perfect parents. Forgiveness in the home may mean children forgiving parents for mistakes as well as parents forgiving children. Until parents and teenagers recognize their mutual sinfulness and need for forgiveness and mercy from each other, the full potential of the healing effect of forgiveness cannot be realized.

The How of Forgiveness

Recognizing the sinfulness of every member of the household does not guarantee the *presence* of forgiveness. As sinful people, we build walls in our relationships. In one situation, a father may sin by hitting his teenage son and later feel so ashamed that he lost his temper that he cannot speak to his son. The son takes the silence as further anger, and a wall is built. In another situation, a daughter says some harsh words to her mother, and the mother is crushed and cries alone in her room; a wall is built.

Few of us have difficulty realizing the need for forgiveness or the presence of sin in the home. It is carrying out the needed forgiveness that becomes awkward. It is dealing with the effects of the sins on our relationships that makes communication break down.

How can that quality of forgiveness be built? For the parent, there are at least four guidelines that must be considered. These can help make the practice of forgiveness an integral part of interaction at home. Although these guidelines are not offered as a cure-all, they may help start the process of healing in broken parent/teen relationships:

1. *Learn to ask for forgiveness.* One of the reasons that teenagers are seldom willing to confront their sins is because they have never seen it done at home. Parents who want healthy relationships at home between themselves and their teenagers (and between their family members and God) must learn to ask for forgiveness.

126

This practice of asking for forgiveness is not just something that happens between the parent and God. The human side of relationships must be dealt with as well. When a parent is tired from a hard day at work, and he snaps at the question of a teenage daughter, the parent should be willing to ask for forgiveness. Unwillingness to listen, snap judgments, and defensiveness are parental sins in relating to teenagers, and the growing parent should be willing to admit these and ask for forgiveness as needed.

This parent/teen openness is something that most parents will find very difficult. Adopting a practice such as asking for forgiveness is very humbling, but it is a God-given criterion for healthy relationships.

"But you don't know my kid!" exclaim some parents. This is true. Not all teenagers will respond the same way to parents' vulnerability, but this does not excuse the parents from holding up their half of the relationship. An atmosphere of mercy and forgiveness must be created by humble parents who are first willing to let others forgive them.

How to get started? A parent who is prone to angry outbursts might start by asking for forgiveness for lack of self-control. Imagine the shock on the face of the teenager who just carelessly drove the car over the hedge when the father replies, "Right now, Bill, I am too angry to deal with the problem. Please go sit in the kitchen. When I get control of my anger, I will talk with you about your problem."

Another way to get started might be an evaluation session, perhaps on the teenager's birthday. When possible, Mother and Dad should take the teen out for lunch. Over lunch, ask this question: "What could we do to be better parents?" Let the teenager talk. Maybe you have hurt your son this year and need to ask forgiveness. Maybe your daughter has some good suggestions for making family life more loving. *Listen.*

One final word about parents asking for forgiveness: Learn to ask for forgiveness without always qualifying your actions or words. "I'm sorry, but I had a lot on my mind." "Forgive me for missing your game, Sandy, but something came up." Forgiveness does not mean excusing your behavior (or worse, blaming it on someone else); forgiveness means confessing your failure and allowing the other person to grant the mercy that is needed.

2. *Forgive and forget.* Psalm 103:12 tells us: "As far as the east is from the west"—that is how far God promises to remove our sins from us. Our problem in interaction is not that we cannot forgive; it is that we cannot forget. Parents have great difficulty forgiving the extreme pain caused by a harsh accusation from a teenager. The ungratefulness of some young people during a rebellious period brings out anger—not forgiveness—in most parents.

Bitterness and grudges do not have a place in Christian relationships, and parents must set the pace at home. True forgiveness starts when a parent is willing to forgive the son or daughter even before being asked. It continues when the person forgiving allows the offender a fresh start, a second chance. It manifests itself in the parent who is willing to bury past failures and not hold them against the young person in the future.

In one family, the daughter confessed to stealing

money from her mother's budget books. The mother forgave—but failed to forget. Several years later, the daughter received a large financial gift for college, which the parents put into an account with only their names on it. When the daughter asked why, the mother told her that since the day of the confession about stealing, she had not felt comfortable trusting her daughter with money. The lack of forgiving and forgetting divided the mother and daughter.

In another family, the eldest son was given responsibility to watch two siblings in the department store. In about thirty minutes, he had managed to lose them both. The teenage son was very fearful as the names were called out over the loudspeaker. Both siblings and the mother appeared at the counter at the same time. Mother listened to the excuses, but finally the son said, "I am sorry, Mom, I blew it."

She responded with forgiveness, and she promptly told her son that she still had a few more errands. "Let's try again," she said, and in saying this, she demonstrated to her son that she was willing to forgive and forget and to give a second chance.

Someone has rewritten a famous saying in this way: TO FORGIVE IS HUMAN, TO FORGET DIVINE. Perhaps it is true: Forgetting is much more difficult than forgiving, but when we remember that God "remembers our sins no more" (see Jer. 31:34), we can be empowered to do the same with others.

3. *Forgive yourself.* I am not a psychologist, but I have observed one very poignant fact about parents with teenagers: Parents are most fearful and overprotective of their teenagers in the realms of life in which

they themselves fell short as teenagers. The parent who cheated as a teen will pressure his son to study hard and never cheat. The parent who felt that she "went to far" sexually as a teenager will pressure her daughter to stay away from boys.

When it comes to forgiveness, some parents need to take a hard look at their own youth. Until we realize that God forgives us for our past sins and failures, we will be subjective in our dealings with teenagers. (I say "we" because I have found the same tendency in myself as a youth leader; I am overcautious toward the youths in my group in the areas I sinned most as a teenager.)

Forgiving ourselves means that we accept the love and mercy of God. We accept the forgiveness, and we believe that God, through Christ, has made us clean. He has forgotten our sins, and we should let them die.

This conscious act of not remembering the sins of our youth (see Ps. 25:7) helps eliminate a subjective blur in the eyes of parents. When our past is forgiven and the sins are forgotten, we see youths as they are rather than under the shadow of our past. This not only helps the teenager get a fresh start; it also relieves the parent of unnecessary suspicion.

This is one area in which Dan and Joan have failed. When they were engaged, they were too involved sexually; she conceived, and they were married quickly. Now, seventeen years later, their daughter, Lori, is dating. Dan puts unreasonable demands on her, forcing her to be home at 9:00 P.M. on weekend nights, never letting her talk privately with her boyfriend, and punishing her severely for even the smallest violation of rules. The irony is that Lori is a committed

Christian, desires to obey her dad, and wants to do what is right, but her father's paranoia ("perhaps she'll make the same mistake I did") is causing their relationship to break down. If only Dan would let God forgive his past and let Lori live in the present, not under the shadow of *his* sins, the relationship would improve.

4. *Forgiveness is not license.* Talking of forgiveness and mercy like this makes many Christian parents quite nervous because they fear that they will become too permissive, never disciplining their children. This is a mistaken concept of mercy that should be corrected.

Admitting that you fail, forgiving and forgetting, and releasing your past do not mean that you give your teenagers free license to sin and break your rules and God's rules. If *mercy* is defined, as "giving someone what he needs, not what he deserves," there is plenty of room for forgiveness in the context of stern discipline. Teenagers need to know that breaking the rules has consequences. Forgiving and covering up consequences could be a big mistake for parents.

The mistakes of youth are to be expected, but these mistakes can be valuable learning experiences if handled correctly. To do this, however, consider these responses:

- When your teenager sins, forgive him from the heart.
- In dealing with the sin, consider the response.
- If the teen is repentant, take this into consideration in your discipline. If the teen is rebellious, you might need to be more severe.

- If there is to be a penalty (maybe the confession is penalty enough), make sure it fits the crime: in other words, grounding the teen for the summer for failing to take out the trash would be too severe.
- If your teen has to go to another person to be reconciled, be willing to go with him or her to offer your support.
- Make sure your emotions are under control, for "the wrath of man does not produce the righteousness of God" (James 1:20). If they are not, wait before dealing with your teen's problem.
- After forgiveness and penalty (if any), let your teen know that your love is unchanged. Be willing to forget the sin and not bring it up again. One parent suggests a hug or a verbal "I love you" after the penalty is over.

Forgiveness and discipline are not mutually exclusive. Instead, they should go hand in hand with growth and learning from mistakes. The toughest assignment of the parent will always be determining how to communicate best both the mercy of God and the discipline of the Spirit to the growing teenager.

Now, Get Started!

One of the most difficult aspects of this matter of forgiveness is that there are no guaranteed answers. Each family and teenager will respond to some of these guidelines differently. The real problems, however, occur in the parents or family who want all of the answers before getting started. Unfortunately, waiting for these answers will mean that the quality of forgiveness and the reality of mercy may never have a chance to enter the home.

The point is this: *Get started*. Start incorporating forgiveness and mercy into your family life. Start asking forgiveness when you sin. Yes, there will be some awkward moments ahead; there will be unanswered questions. But until you start bringing mercy into your home, there will be a lack in your family relationships.

The father in the Beatles' song responds with apathy to a runaway daughter; the mother responds with self-pity. Neither is the correct response to failure. To maximize effectiveness in the Christian home, sins must be confronted with the power of the mercy of God. By so doing, family members can receive the forgiveness they need for growth.

Conclusion

Healthy relationships between parents and teenagers are possible. I know because I have seen parents and teenagers who are growing together. The principles of this book can be put into practice, and families can flourish as a result. The challenge is great, but so are the rewards.

Healthy relationships yield healthy teenagers, and healthy teenagers can grow to mature adulthood and be effective husbands, wives, parents, and leaders in the next generation. We have everything to gain in the church, the home, and the society-at-large by investing in our teenagers.

For the parent who is still asking, "Where do I start?" consider three steps:

1. *Do a family evaluation.* Force discussion between yourself and your teenager. Ask some questions: "Do you feel loved?"; "Have I been helping you grow?"; "Where would you like to see changes here at home?"

Be aware, however, that if you ask direct questions, you may get some direct answers! The evaluation may not be easy, but it is the best place to start because it will tell you where changes might be needed at the outset, at least from your teenager's perspective.

The evaluation should take place between husbands and wives as well. In the case of the single parent, consider asking a close adult friend to observe your family for a few days and to share what he or she learns with you. This type of evaluation can yield observations about protective fathers, bossy mothers, or a general fear of what the teenager is becoming.

The evaluation may not result in solutions; it may actually reveal more problem areas, but it will serve to show parents where to start working. It can also bring parents to the point of prayer as they recognize that issues needing correction may be bigger than they can handle alone.

2. *Get to know your teenager.* In several chapters, qualities or issues were discussed that required the parent to know the world of the teenager. This is a great challenge for you as a parent because it involves the skills of an international worker in the area of cross-cultural adaptation. The music, language, clothing styles, and values might be very hard for you to understand, but knowing where your teenager lives will help build better communication.

Knowing your teenager means more than just knowing adolescent culture. It means knowing *your own* son or daughter. What are his dreams for the future? What things really mean the most to her? In what ways is she like you? In what ways is he different?

Understanding your teenager is the best way to start building healthier, more meaningful relationships. And, for the openminded parent, there will even be a lot to be learned about yourself in the process.

3. *Take some positive steps.* The worst response a parent can make to a book like this is to say, "It is all too overwhelming; I feel so far behind as a parent that I want to give up!"

Do Not Give Up

Start where you are. If you are out of touch with your teenager, then start making small steps toward improving that relationship. If things have been disintegrating over the past five years, don't expect immediate healing in five days. Start small. Work consistently. And *please* do not give up.

Parents who start taking positive steps can see poor relationships improve and good relationships get better. No parent is ready to take all ten of these chapters and do an instant, total overhaul of the family. Growth takes time, and the process of growth is a matter of moving in a positive direction. Take some positive steps to affirm your love, to give some responsibility, to show your respect. The little steps will start to yield some improvements in relationships, and growth can continue.

A Chinese proverb states that "even the greatest journey begins with a single step." Start the journey of building a healthier relationship with your teenager by taking that first step, then the second, and the third, and so on. One step at a time will result in covering much of the road toward growth over a period of time and effort. Start now, and don't give up.

"But you don't understand"?

Well, maybe you do!

Suggested Reading List

Blamires, Harry. *The Christian Mind*. Ann Arbor, Mich.: Servant Publications, 1978.

Buntman, Peter H., and E. M. Saris. *How to Live with Your Teenagers*. Pasadena: Birch Tree Press, 1982.

Bustanoby, Andre. *The Ready-Made Family*. Grand Rapids: Zondervan, 1982.

Campbell, Ross. *How to Really Love Your Child*. New York: New American Library, 1982.

Davitz, Lois and Joel. *How to Live (Almost) Happily with a Teenager*. Minneapolis: Winston Press, 1982.

DiGiacomo, James, and Edward Wakin. *Understanding Teenagers: A Guide for Parents*. Allen, Tex.: Argus Books, 1983.

Dobson, James. *Preparing for Adolescence*. New York: Bantam, 1980.

Elkind, David. *All Grown Up and No Place to Go*. Reading, Mass.: Addison-Wesley, 1984.

Ellul, Jacques. *Money and Power*. Downers Grove, Ill.: InterVarsity Press, 1984.

Farel, Anita M. *Early Adolescence: What Parents Need to Know*. Carrboro, N.C.: Center for Early Adolescence.

Glenbard East *Echo,* compilation. *Teenagers Themselves.* New York: Adama Books, 1984.

Johnson, Rex. *Communication: Key to Your Parents.* Irvine, Calif.: Harvest House, 1978.

Kesler, Jay. *Let's Succeed with Our Teenagers.* Elgin, Ill.: David C. Cook, 1973.

————. *Too Big to Spank.* Glendale, Calif.: Regal Books, 1978.

————, ed. *Parents and Teenagers.* Wheaton: Victor Books, 1984.

Keyes, Ralph. *Is There Life After High School?* New York: Warner, 1976.

Kolb, Erwin J. *Parents Guide to Conversations about Sex.* St. Louis: Concordia Press, 1980.

Lewis, Margie. *The Hurting Parent.* Grand Rapids: Zondervan, 1980.

MacDonald, Gordon. *The Effective Father.* Wheaton, Ill.: Tyndale, 1977.

Norman, Jane, and Myron Harris. *The Private Life of an American Teenager.* New York: Rawson-Wade, 1981.

Oraker, James. *Almost Grown.* New York: Harper and Row, 1980.

Poure, Ken. *Parents: Give Your Kid a Chance.* Irvine, Calif.: Harvest House Publishers, 1977.

Ridenour, Fritz. *What Teenagers Wish Their Parents Knew About Kids.* Waco, Tex.: Word, 1983.

Rushford, Patricia H. *Have You Hugged Your Teenager Today?* Old Tappan, N.J.: Fleming H. Revell, 1983.

Stafford, Tim. *The Trouble with Parents.* Wheaton: Campus Life Books, 1978.

Strommen, Merton P. *Five Cries of Parents.* New York: Harper and Row, 1985.

_____ . *Five Cries of Youth*. New York: Harper and Row, 1974.

Wells, Joel. *How to Survive with Your Teenager*. Chicago: Thomas Moore Press, 1982.

White, John. *Parents in Pain*. Downers Grove, Ill.: Inter-Varsity Press, 1979.

Wilkerson, Rich. *Hold Me While You Let Me Go*. Eugene, Ore.: Harvest House, 1979.

Wilson, Earl D. *You Try Being a Teenager: To Parents to Stay in Touch*. Portland, Ore.: Multnomah Press, 1982.

Wright, Norman, and Rex Johnson. *Communication: Key to Your Teenagers*. Irvine, Calif.: Harvest House, 1978.

A-1